The Pursuit of Fairness:

Fighting for What's **Right** in a World That's So **Wrong**

ALAN L. JENNINGS

Allentown, PA

Copyright © 2019 Alan L. Jennings
Registration Number: TXu 2-163-090
All Rights Reserved. Published by Rocky Rapids Press.

No part of this publication may be reproduced, stored in a retrieval system, or tansmitted in any form or by any means, electronic, mechanical, photocopying, recording, or otherwise without permission of the publisher.

ISBN: 978-1-7320636-2-4

Cover photograph by *The Morning Call*.

Backcover photograph by Keenan-Nagle Advertising, Inc.

www.caclv.org

Dedication

To my wife, Denise, who keeps me grounded and who never signed up for the cause but may have sacrificed the most.

And our children, Stephanie, Greer and Haley, whose world I worked my ass off to improve but who paid a price while I tried.

And our grandchildren, Zeke, Xander and Sophie, who don't deserve the world they'll be handed.

Oh, and, Jesus, who led the way but, like me, failed.

Finally, this book is dedicated to anyone who's ever wondered whether the world can be saved.

Acknowledgements

I'd love to acknowledge everyone who ever helped me try to make a difference, but that would basically require me to name everyone but a few jerks who fought hard to block every attempt to do something good. But that's not what "acknowledgements" means, anyway. I'm pretty sure it means the folks who helped me put this book together, so here goes:

Eric Arnson
Wayne Barz
Janine Slaughter
Zach Cobrinik
Linda Faust
Tom Garrity
Mike Gausling
Maryann Haytmanek
Sharol Lilly
Charlie Marcon

Susan Moore
Janet Ney
Ludwig Schlecht
Robb and Lydia Turner
Todd Watkins
Roger Yott
David Erdman
Paul Pierpoint
The Honorable Robert Young

Eric Arnson and Bob Young deserve special thanks. They both believed in this project and committed the time, talent and treasure to make it happen.

Table of Contents

INTRODUCTION . . . . The Value of Picking Fights i

SECTION I . . . . A MAN ON A HILL 1

    CHAPTER 1 . . . . Hi, I'm Alan Jennings 3

    CHAPTER 2 . . . . The Stage Gets Set 10

    CHAPTER 3 . . . . Divine Intervention 13

    CHAPTER 4 . . . . I Hope This Book Gives You Hope 19

    CHAPTER 5 . . . . The Starting Point 22

    CHAPTER 6 . . . . Institutional Vehicles For Promoting Change 24

    CHAPTER 7 . . . . Whatever You Call It, Do It 25

    CHAPTER 8 . . . . Community Action Agencies 29

SECTION II . . . . HELP, THEY NEED SOMEBODY 33

    CHAPTER 9 . . . . Nonprofits and Their Boards of Directors 35

    CHAPTER 10 . . . . So, You're Clean? Check Again 47

    CHAPTER 11 . . . . Fundraising 50

    CHAPTER 12 . . . . Don't Call Me "President and CEO"
                      and Other Lessons We Shouldn't Learn the Hard Way 57

    CHAPTER 13 . . . . . . Where Did You Get the Idea That Lobbying Was Illegal? 60

    CHAPTER 14 . . . . The Community Reinvestment Act 65

CHAPTER 15 . . . . .Advocacy 81

CHAPTER 16 . . . . .Raising Hell and Raising Money, Too 89

CHAPTER 17 . . . . .There Are Plenty of Ways to Do It 94

CHAPTER 18 .Marx Was Wrong On At Least This Issue 97

CHAPTER 19 . . . . .Good Customer Service in an Era When
"Good Customer Service" is an Oxymoron 103

SECTION III . . . . THE LONG AND REALLY WINDING ROAD 109

CHAPTER 20 . . . . .They Fight Poverty, Don't They? 111

CHAPTER 21 . . How the Mainstream Media Work and How You Can Use It 113

CHAPTER 22 . . . . .Taking On a Consensus Bad Guy: The Slum Landlord 124

CHAPTER 23 . . . . I Wish I'd Made This Up 132

CHAPTER 24 . . . . .Lest You Think It's Been All Successes and No Failures… 144

CHAPTER 25 . . . ."He's Only Happy When He's Fighting Mad" 146

CHAPTER 26 . . . . .Got A World View? Get One! 148

CHAPTER 27 . . . . Jenningsisms: The Words We Choose 157

CHAPTER 28 . . . . The Words We Choose, Part 2 159

CHAPTER 29 . . . . . . .Advice For the Activist Without Institutional Ramparts 161

SECTION IV . . . . **IN MY LIFE 163**

CHAPTER 30 . . . ."The Rap on You Is, You're Manipulative" 165

CHAPTER 31 . . . . "The Only Thing in the Middle of the Road in This Country is Dead Armadillos and Yellow Stripes" – Jim Hightower 167

CHAPTER 32 . . . . And Here's Where I Am 170

CHAPTER 33 . . . . Did You Get the Main Points? 173

CHAPTER 34 . . . . Don't Give Up 175

Epilogue . . . ."There Comes a Redeemer…" 176

Appendices 179

Introduction

The Value of Picking Fights

THE GUY HAD TO GO.

Mr. Jones, as we'll call him, was the executive director of a local public housing authority was the stereotype of the plantation owner as housing authority director. Mr. Jones had it all going on. He considered himself progressive because residents got to pick which shade of tan paint they liked as the color of their walls.

Depending on the circumstances, I would try to work with him and would inevitably end up giving up. The guy wanted to be seen as an achiever. He just couldn't pull it off, mostly because he had that control-freak plantation-owner mindset.

At the time the U.S. Department of Housing and Urban Development provided funding to public housing authorities to raze obsolete, blighted federal housing projects like Robert Taylor Homes in Chicago. These projects were monuments to failed federal housing policy that "ghetto-ized" poor people. The new new HUD program, called HOPE VI, financed new, better-planned neighborhoods in their place. These new neighborhoods mixed low-income rental housing, rentals for seniors and single-family homes for owner-occupancy. HOPE VI was conceived by Jack Kemp, former NFL quarterback who went on to represent Buffalo in the U.S. House of Representatives, when he served President George H.W. Bush as his HUD secretary.

Our region had already been successful in obtaining the very competitive funding for a project in a nearby city. That meant getting funding for this second project would be all the more challenging. That didn't stop Mr. Jones, who fancied himself capable of pulling off a miracle. The problem was that he needed to demonstrate that he was capable of successfully implementing a project of this significance. Succeeding meant engaging partners who could help develop the critically-important services needed to help residents break the cycle of poverty.

I offered to help, thinking that we could improve conditions for the residents by getting them better housing as well as strengthening services designed to help them become more self-sufficient, and we would improve the nearby neighborhood as well. He accepted. I brought together a bunch of organizations ranging from groups that could do casework to the local job training agency and the community college. We also offered to do community organizing designed to engage residents in solving their own problems, which was consistent with the style and approach championed by Secretary Kemp.

GACK! COMMUNITY ORGANIZING?!! You'd think I'd suggested that poor people actually be empowered to call their own shots. Mr. Jones pounded his fist on the table and, essentially, told us all to drop dead. We promptly dropped out and Mr. Jones had to submit an utterly inadequate proposal that had no chance of being funded. He wasted a bunch of money to hire a consultant to submit the proposal that was doomed to fail.

It did.

Mr. Jones tried again. This time, we refused to assist. He failed again, wasting still more money on consultants who couldn't put together a decent project without us. By this time the press was running stories about this silly charade. That gave us an opening.

We went to meetings of the commissioners of the housing authority, not normally meetings the press would bother to cover. They covered these, though; they were becoming a circus. At one meeting one of the commissioners called a reporter a "bitch," saying it loud enough to be heard where I was sitting. I immediately jumped up and called on the offending commissioner to resign. Cameras rolled, pens scribbled. This was getting more interesting every day.

Then Mr. Jones proposed yet again that the housing authority spend a bunch more money on yet another attempt to compete for HOPE VI funding. We made it clear that we would only assist if Mr. Jones stepped down. By this point, his behavior was getting more erratic and nonsensical, making ridiculous claims and lying about my role. We could tell he was getting close to the breaking point.

Finally, he laid out one more rant at a public meeting, personally attacking me. And then he announced that he'd had enough. And it was over.

We then stepped up and put together an outstanding proposal. We lobbied Rick Santorum, at the time the junior U.S. Senator from Pennsylvania, who needed desperately to look effective and like he cared more about poor people and their neighborhoods than his record indicated because he was increasingly looking like he was going to lose his campaign for re-election. He worked HUD and successfully put the icing on the cake that got us the hoped-for HOPE VI funding.

There is no real lesson here, unlike most of the stories in this book that illustrate the how-to stuff. But it does illustrate what a brash punk I can be, even in my mid-40's. It demonstrates how bare-knuckled we can be when a figurative fist fight is the only option left. It also pointed out that sometimes the fight, won or lost, can be the desired outcome by sending a clear message to all current and future bad guys that fighting with us was pretty risky.

Real people are too unwilling to pick these fights. And that's just one of the reasons why we as a nation of communities are making so little progress.

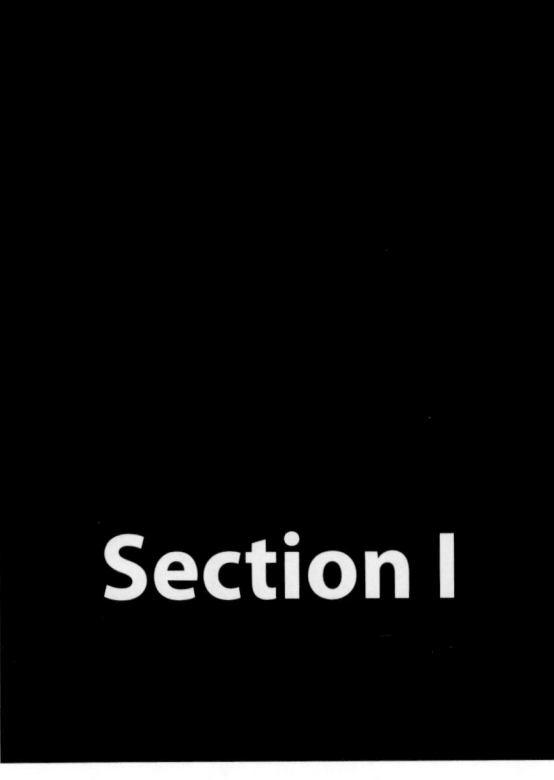

Section I

A Man on a Hill

Chapter 1

Hi, I'm Alan Jennings

I HAVE A VERY CLEAR PERSPECTIVE ON WHO I AM. I KNOW HOW FLAWED I AM. I KNOW HOW GOOD I CAN BE. I am blunt to a fault, driven to distress, profane, obsessed, annoying and persistent. Lots of people hate me. The local blogs are jammed with people lined up to excoriate me for having the nerve to give a shit. F*ck them. (Did I mention profane?) In many ways, most of my character traits are curses. They are also gifts. I couldn't do what I do without them.

Actually, I want to be judged at least as much by who my enemies are as by who my friends are. Lest you think I really like having countless detractors, I try very hard to have many times more of the latter as the former. In fact, when people tell me I'm either loved or hated, my response is usually to come close to begging for names of the latter. Undoubtedly, some of the folks in the "hate" column are probably people about whom I care and whose opinions matter to me. If I knew those individuals were, indeed, in the hate column, I'd make a special effort to win them over, if at all possible.

I should probably be working as an assistant manager of an Enterprise Rental Car store. There isn't a shred of privilege in my life.

Believe that? You shouldn't. I grew up in the suburbs. I'm a Presbyterian. Something my parents did (unwittingly, I'm sure), or something deep inside of my consciousness, made me a dangerously driven person. And somewhere along the way I picked up a pretty good intellect. Thanks to financial aid, I was able to go to a respectable college (Dickinson College in Carlisle, Pennsylvania).

The bottom line is that I'm just some guy. A white guy. Nothing about me suggests I am anything more than a regular white guy. No special schooling, no special connections, no trust fund. Just a regular guy burning to make a difference. A guy who got a job at a non-profit that gave me a trajectory, enabling me to chase the expectations I felt He placed on me; and, of course, to tell the story.

That's why we are here. That's what this book is about.

Maybe I can help a few people learn a bit. Maybe I can inspire someone. Maybe give you hope. Maybe give you the notion that you can pursue your dreams and someday look back and mutter, "I hope I made a difference."

If you're serious enough to take this ride with me, you ought to know what you're getting yourself into.

People are always asking how I got to be the way I am. The question always makes me smirk.

The defining elements of the guy whose work for whatever reason you are reading right now, are as follows.

I'M A MIDDLE CHILD
Seriously. My older brother got all of the privileges, my younger brother all of the attention. When you're a middle child, nothing is fair. Or, maybe I should say that fairness became, for me, the meter by which everything else in my life was measured.

THE GOLDEN RULE
I mean the traditional version, not "He who has the gold makes the rules."

My mother, a working class woman with a shaky educational record and without a shred of pretension, pounded the Golden Rule into me. She said it so many times I had it memorized by the time they cut the umbilical cord.

If you take that rule to its logical extreme, it takes empathy to its extreme -- everyone else's suffering becomes your own. And I'll be damned if I am going to suffer. So, I'm fighting back, standing with the oppressed, with the marginalized, with the left out. I hated how Charlie Brown was knocked down. I got between the bully and his victim. When choosing sides for our backyard football or baseball games, or any other game I was always organizing, I often picked the kid who was likely to be picked last earlier so he didn't get picked last.

MY FATHER WAS AN ALCOHOLIC

I have never gotten a professional's opinion, much less counseling, on this issue, but my father was an embarrassing drunk. His words were always slurred. He'd claim he had just one beer. He lost three jobs in barely five years. He fell on Christmas Eve, drunk, of course, and spent the holiday in the hospital. He lost over $100 one night which, in the 1960's, was a lot more money than it is today.

He died at 51, when I was 15. I can't say that I have ever missed him.

MY MOTHER HAD NO SENSE OF THE POSSIBILITIES…

"Why are you going out for sports? You know you're not an athlete!"

Most kids would have had no self-esteem. Really, Mom? I became the first captain of my high school volleyball team and the first all-league (OK, it was the second team, but I'll take it) player from my high school.

"Why are you running for office? You don't think you're going to win, do you?"

As a freshman at Dickinson College I ran for school board in my home district. My grand scheme was to be the youngest school director in Pennsylvania, run for and become the youngest state representative when I was in my mid-twenties, the youngest United States congressman in my early thirties, and a U.S. senator a few terms after that.

I lost by 49 votes on the Republican ballot (I cross-filed), more on the Democratic ballot. I never thought to send absentee ballots to my friends in colleges all across the country. That plan was thwarted. OK, so Mom was right this time. But I wonder how much of what I write in this book would have been different had that 1977 election gone another way.

The point is, most kids' dreams would be crushed by a parent setting the bar so low. Not me. It was probably what motivated me the most.

…AND HER CLASS CONSCIOUSNESS WAS UNCOMPROMISING

My mother was openly hostile toward class, privilege and the many ways they were manifested in our lives and culture. It wasn't a reasoned or educated perspective; it was just pure resentment. And she fed mine.

As an aside, my wife and I and, at the time, two kids were driving somewhere and my older daughter, Stephanie, who might have been 6, says, "I know why people are poor." "Why, Stephanie?" "Because some people have too much." If a 6-year-old can figure that one out, why can't the rest of us?

MY OLDER BROTHER, MARK

I don't think any other single person had a more profound effect on my life. He was nearly 10 years older than I. He was a musician, wouldn't get a haircut, made sure we watched the Beatles on the Ed Sullivan Show in February, 1964. The times were getting increasingly contentious and I had a front row seat.

He introduced me to the angry angst of The Kinks. In fact, the first of hundreds of concerts I have seen was a Kinks/Beach Boys concert in 1972, when I was 14.

When the local high schools called in their weekly top three hits to the AM radio station, my brother's rock group, The Shillings, were on the list (the feature was called "The High School Hotline"). Our whole neighborhood gathered in a neighbor's house to watch The Shillings on the Steel Pier Show out of Atlantic City. Mark introduced me to marijuana at age 13. I paid much more attention to the counter-culture, Viet Nam (he got a medical deferment), and the civil rights movement because of him. I was in awe.

I have a younger brother, too: Kevin. We are not particularly close and we fought a lot. I do admit that the way that I treated him raises serious questions about whether I have any legitimate claim to common decency.

THE SIXTIES
I was only five when I watched Jack Ruby shoot Lee Harvey Oswald on live television; six when the Beatles arrived; nine when LBJ announced that he would not seek, nor, if nominated, accept his party's nomination as a candidate for re-election. I was nearly 10 when the Rev. Dr. Martin Luther King, Jr., was shot in Memphis, 10 when Bobby Kennedy was shot in Los Angeles. I was 11 when a half-million hippies descended on Max Yasgur's farm near Woodstock, New York, and Neil Armstrong set foot on the moon. I had that DayGlo Dylan poster and the black-and-white Einstein poster. I was 14 when the Watergate scandal broke.

Because my brother was in the middle of the counter-culture and my father insisted we quiet down when Chet Huntley and David Brinkley were presenting the news, I was paying far more attention than any of my friends. They were oblivious. I was hip.

Then there was the music. Without a doubt, the 1960's were the most significant cultural breakthrough in history. It provided my life with a soundtrack. I saw "A Hard Day's Night" and "Dr. Strangelove" at the Colonial Theater in Allentown. I listened to every Beatles song over and over. The Beach Boys, the Zombies, Gerry and the Pacemakers, the Dave Clark Five. Motown. American Bandstand, Hullabaloo, Shindig, Laugh-in, The Monkees. I remember the labels on the 45s. "It's a Beautiful Day," "Mad Dogs and Englishmen," Buffalo Springfield, Sly and the Family Stone. I cried when the rumors circulated that Paul was dead.

RACE
My vacations were spent visiting family in Hagerstown, Maryland. As we drove through the "colored" part of town, my parents told us to roll our windows up.

As a kid obsessed with fairness, nothing compares to the black experience. In my extremist empathy, I felt black. I'm not going to suffer, damn it.

I admit that the Black Panthers scared the hell out of me. But, then again, they never lynched anyone.

I BROKE THE RULES
In fact, I'm not even sure I respected many of them enough to believe they applied to me.

I HAD A FEELING
Here is where you might think I'm more than a little looney. I was in my parents' bedroom, maybe 7 or 8 years old. I remember standing in front of their full-length mirror. As I stood there, I became overwhelmed by a feeling that God had expectations of me. I mean, serious expectations. I remember feeling (I never heard a voice) that God had placed expectations on me that I make a heroic difference. I felt chosen. I can't explain it. And I would understand if you think I was one crazy-assed kid. But I went through the next 35 years carrying the burden of trying to have the kind of impact my heroes had.

The problem was that my heroes were such a threat to the status quo that most were dead by age 40: MLK, Robert Kennedy, Jesus. As I approached my late 30s it became apparent that I wasn't going to meet those great expectations; I wasn't dead yet. I can't explain how much pressure I felt to meet God's expectations, and how depressed I was with the realization that I wouldn't.

IT SHOULDN'T SURPRISE YOU THAT I HAVE OTHER ISSUES
My poor parents; I was born anti-authoritarian. I tend to ignore rules that don't improve the common good. I respect most people, those who have and those who have not, those who can and those who cannot, black, brown, or white, left or right, with power or without. Nobody intimidates me. You could call that stupid, you could call that too ignorant to know better. You could accuse me of not being raised properly. I must have Adult Attention Deficit Disorder. I can't pay attention to anything for very

Did I tell you about my propensity for empathy? It is almost crippling.

In a world where some have so much it haunts me that so many have so little.

It puzzles me that so few who are successful appreciate the degree to which luck factored into their success; by contrast, it might sadden me more that people are so beaten down that they have no expectations of themselves.

People compromise their faith to take advantage of the good fortune that comes their way. And it always amazes me how selective some people can be about some of the most basic of values even a cursory read of the Bible makes quite clear.

I think I have some kind of natural ability to understand the nexus of politics and economics and their effect on our world.

I have loose threads hanging all over the place, an outcome of working at a frenetic pace for 35 years. Those loose threads are project ideas that are somewhere between a twinkle in my eye and waiting for money to appear out of dirt. I wish we had the resources to tie those threads together.

Sometimes I think I take too many risks. Other times I get angry with myself for not taking one.

MOST OF ALL, DENISE REYNOLDS
No boy and girl could be more different. But when I was 14, I sought out this cute, shy, blond. She crushed me when she broke up with me, twice. She'd say, no, "So sorry for not wanting to get married when we were 16." I couldn't imagine my life without her. She saved me from all kinds of stupidity. She refined me. She tempered me. Sort of.

Chapter 2

The Stage Gets Set

DICKINSON COLLEGE HELPED ME PUT MY ANGER INTO CONTEXT, HISTORICALLY, CULTURALLY, POLITICALLY, ECONOMICALLY. All those privileged (read: lucky) kids in their Docksiders (I'd never seen a pair of those geeky shoes before I got to Dickinson), prep-school-educated, oblivious to the world's troubles, spending as much money on cocaine in one night as my poor mother could afford to give me to spend in an entire semester, further sharpened my anger.

A bunch of my friends studied in Bologna, Italy, during our junior year. Bologna was the seat of Euro-communism, the home of the terrorist Red Brigade. Most of those who participated in the program, including the spoiled rich kids, came back radicalized. I tried to seize the opportunity.

I got some of them who I thought might be interested together to talk about doing some kind of radical action. We met off-campus, locked the doors, turned the music up loud, just in case the FBI was listening.

I had an anarchistic streak that favored disruption. I proposed blowing up a train moving new cars from Detroit to market, but only if we could be assured there would be no injuries. No support. I backed off a little, forcefully making the case for hijacking a fuel oil truck and distributing the contents to poor folks in Carlisle. I thought this was a good one. You know, Robin Hood, the hated oil industry. Nobody gets hurt. No takers.

We settled on a wimpy demonstration in front of the ROTC building to protest President Carter's imposition of the selective service system in response to the

Soviet invasion of Afghanistan. The faculty who joined us outnumbered the students. Many students muttered "communist" when they walked through our picket line. Pay attention, this will be a recurring story: I made sure the press knew about the event.

A few months later I called in a bomb threat to the Democratic National Convention from a pay phone across the street from Madison Square Garden in New York. I told them I was with a rightwing extremist group called something like the National Front. It was a defiant, fist-in-the-air, anarchistic act of stupidity and it scared the shit out of me. I was an idiot. Fortunately, that's the last really stupid thing I did for the cause. Note: lots of people probably would disagree with that.

I was a radical. I used to say that if I hadn't been married with a precious little daughter, I would have gone to Nicaragua and joined the Sandinistas.

I graduated from Dickinson College in May, 1980. Denise and I, with our first-born, Stephanie, on the way, were married on April 27.

I didn't have a job (luckily, Denise had graduated with a two-year degree and was managing at a local department store). But I was called for federal jury duty in Philadelphia the day after I picked up my degree in political science. As seriously as I took my civic duty, the timing was awful. I didn't want to serve on a sequestered jury, so I made sure those scrutinizing the jury panels knew I was far too opinionated to serve. I carried around my paperback copy of "Fear and Loathing on the Campaign Trail" by Hunter S. Thompson. The cover had a drawing of a skull, American flag imposed on it, with swastikas in the eye sockets.

One day, we were sent to Reading about 60 miles outside of Philly. We were told nothing, directed to a windowless room with a guard outside. There was a rumor that we were there for jury selection in the corruption trial of U.S. Dan Flood, from Scranton. Instead of sitting on a panel and being questioned collectively, we were brought into the courtroom one by one. We sat in the witness stand. The federal judge presided. I recognized nationally-known lawyer Richard Sprague, who had served the Warren Commission in its investigation of the Kennedy assassination. I told them I knew for what trial they were choosing jurors. They asked me if I had an opinion. I told them that, of course I did. I said, though, that Flood was no more guilty than an entire system that was corrupt, favoring the few, neglecting the many. I barely finished the sentence when one of the attorneys moved that I be dismissed. Close one!

My empathy was easily converted to anger along the way. You get knocked around long enough, believing you're the victim like those whose pain you shared, and you get pretty pissed. Billy Joel's "Angry Young Man" was thematic.

It was 1980, a terrible year to enter the labor market. The economy was heading for disaster. Plus, I refused to work for The Man. I only applied for jobs that didn't require selling out. God bless Denise for tolerating me.

Then again, we desperately needed income. So, I took a job making steak sandwiches and subs.

Among the many, many jobs for which I applied was a position as coordinator of an employment placement program for a nonprofit called the Community Action Committee of the Lehigh Valley. I had never heard of the organization. I didn't get the $10,500 position but it was only the second interview I had gotten in a field that fit my plans. Progress! They gave the job to a former banker.

They did, though, offer me a lower position as employment counselor in one of three locations in the Lehigh Valley, reporting to the coordinator. I took it. It paid $9,500. It would be located in a dumpy, little storefront on Ridge Avenue in Allentown's poorest neighborhood.

It took me about three days to realize this agency, a remnant of the War on Poverty, could be the illustration President-elect Ronald Reagan needed to prove that "government can't solve problems; government was the problem" or that "we fought a war on poverty and poverty won." Never mind the details; I wasn't impressed.

I was there about a month, hustling to save the world, when I was informed that the banker declined the coordinator's position. Apparently, I had done enough to deserve the offer of the position I originally sought. I accepted, of course. But I had no grand scheme for how I would use this position to save the world. I would just hustle, hustle like a guy who felt God had put him on the planet to make a heroic difference.

Chapter 3

Divine Intervention

IT HAD TO BE.

I was fighting the radical agenda Ronald Reagan was pushing while running my little job placement program. I started at CACLV just 40 days or so after he snagged the White House from Jimmy Carter. Add to that that a bunch of the old liberals were tossed out of the Congress in 1978 and still more in 1980 on Reagan's coattails. Gone were Bayh, Magnuson, Church, Brademas, McGovern and others. Reagan, remember, hated government. And his policies stood in defiance of the values so many of his Christian faith embraced. During the campaign, he proposed cutting all social "welfare" spending by 25 percent and turning as much of the rest over to the states and local government as they could get away with.

But they hated some programs more than others. Notably, funding for three programs dating back to the Johnson Administration's War on Poverty were targeted to be cut to zero: VISTA (a program best known for supporting community organizing), the Legal Services Corporation (providing free legal representation to poor people on civil matters) and, yes, Community Action Agencies, the very cornerstone of the War on Poverty.

The right had called for Reagan to "defund the Left." These three programs were seen as change agent programs and the Right felt that providing government funding to promote changing the status quo was going way too far. When Reagan was governor and Ed Meese his attorney general, the legal services groups in California, many of which were started by or part of Community Action Agencies, were suing the agriculture industry on behalf of migrant workers organized by Chicano organizer Cesar Chavez of the United Farm Workers as well as the nursing home industry on behalf of low-income seniors. VISTA funded community organizing campaigns that had the nerve to engage poor people in the local problem-solving process. Reagan proposed killing their funding altogether. This would be one of those situations where I was proud to be a target, except that the stakes were pretty high.

As an employee of a CAA who had some enthusiasm for the possibilities -- e.g. the difference we could make if we did it right), it was sad to realize how few really cared about the prospect of the Lehigh Valley's CAA being abandoned.

Apparently, though, there were enough worthy CAA's among the 1,000 serving most of the counties in the country to motivate Congressional Democrats to fight the attempt to kill us. The compromise was to cut the program by 25 percent and to turn the remainder over to the states for administration. The Community Services Block Grant (CSBG) was born.

Richard Thornburgh, a moderate former prosecutor from Pittsburgh who was moving right fast with the Reagan (gag me) Revolution, proposed conducting an independent review of the 34 agencies in Pennsylvania. This was, I must admit, a perfectly understandable move on the part of Governor Thornburgh.

The problem was the outcome of the review. They named CACLV as the fourth worst CAA in the Commonwealth. Ouch. Uh, oh. But, frankly, we deserved it.

The good news was that the Reading, Pittsburgh and Philadelphia CAA's came out worse than ours did. Phew! It was pretty unlikely that they would take us down if it meant taking three of Pennsylvania's biggest cities' anti-poverty programs down with them.

We were placed on probation, given a 90-day funding commitment (sans 25 percent) and told to make some decent progress if we wanted to survive past September 30, 1982. That was enough reason for the executive director to bail on the agency.

At the board's annual meeting in June, the board announced that they would shut the agency down October 1 if the probation period was not suspended or extended prior to that. By then, the agency's executive director bailed on his sinking ship.

The Community Action Committee of the Lehigh Valley was in trouble. Unable to offer a new executive director the slightest bit of job security, the board looked internally. I was too noisy, fighting policy battles with the Reagan and Thornburgh administrations. In fact, the board had just had a contentious battle over the board president's insistence on firing me for submitting a sharply-worded opinion column to The Morning Call, the region's top daily newspaper, about the Thornburgh administration's latest effort to cut the state's general assistance program. You see, I did it even though I was told not to submit it. That, you know, is insubordination.

So, a woman on the staff serving in the position of planner was named executive director. She had the news clipping taped on her door for a couple years: "Woman, 24, to head CACLV." She then appointed me to her former position. The headline would have read, "Punk, 24, to take CACLV second spot." Yikes! Two kids running the place!

Was this just crazy luck? It couldn't be – I never have good luck. I'm that guy in the cartoons who always has a dark cloud over his head. This could only be divine intervention.

It was 1982. The Fed would choke the over-heated Carter economy with big increases in the cost of money. The economy was in recession, taking a deep dive with room to decline further. The industrial sector was heaving jobs, plants were being shut down; a major shift in the economy was uprooting everything. Unemployment topped 12 percent.

THIS WAS OUR STRATEGY FOR SAVING THE AGENCY
This economy was cruel. The deindustrialization of the American economy, manifested in the Lehigh Valley as much as any other part of the aging Rust Belt, was wrenching. Tens of thousands of working class families were losing

the wages and benefits of their head of household. Plants were not just heaving workers, they were closing; a pretty good sign they weren't coming back. Here in the Lehigh Valley, Black & Decker, Champion Spark Plugs, Mack Trucks, an assortment of garment factories, and whole chunks of Bethlehem Steel were locking up the gates.

Reagan was even more cruel. No part of the safety net was spared. He hated government, said it couldn't solve problems but was the problem and he was apparently intent on proving it. At a time when the safety net was needed more than at any time before, he was making sure it wouldn't be there.

The guy who stupidly thought that taking out a train would be good, radical tactics, was now working in a relatively mainstream nonprofit. I had my vehicle for stirring up the pot and I was actively fighting the Reagan agenda, especially its budget proposals.

In February, 1982, Ed Meese, probably the Reagan Administration's most visible (and vilified) senior official, was coming to Allentown to campaign for U.S. Representative Don Ritter. The very upscale fundraiser would take place at the Hilton Hotel in downtown Allentown. Ritter's politics seemed pretty extreme for the community where I grew up and I had taken it upon myself to challenge him in every way I could. This $150 per plate event in a community where people's hopes for the promise of America had evaporated seemed particularly illustrative of all that made me such an angry young man.

Ed Meese! That was almost as good as President Reagan himself. We got everybody together, union leaders, human service agencies, human rights activists, faith-based groups, collectively licked our chops and discussed the opportunity presented us. Here was an opportunity to use someone who was a walking, talking political icon who personified the worst of political operatives in the Reagan era. There was no way we were going to let this guy come to town without taking advantage of the opportunity to illustrate how wrong it is to celebrate affluence amidst such despair.

We decided to organize a demonstration. Given how much the political economy of the early 1980s was starting to resemble the early 1930s, maybe even Charles

Dickens' era, let's remind people how wrong such disparity between those who had and those who had not was.

We did a soup line, distributing lentil soup and handing out apples. Some 400 people participated. It got a little out of hand when the crowd started taunting the lucky folks in their Mercedes and Cadillacs, women in their furs. I had nothing to do with that part.

I got my first hit as a target of the editorial writers, criticized for using the "ersatz" (I had to look that one up) symbolism of the Great Depression to attack the policies of those who probably had never met a poor person. I still have the news clippings; I was proud of that one.

Within weeks, the Lehigh Valley was creating soup kitchens. How ersatz is that? Within a year, more than 300 people were being served at a soup kitchen each day. It seemed to me that this was no way to help people in need. Wouldn't a job be better? Or, at least food stamps?

But, apparently, that's what our world had come to. Charity. I hate charity. Charity is what you do when you don't have justice. (That's in our values statement. I swear Bono stole the line from me.)

It didn't take much to project out what high unemployment and a tattered safety net would mean for our community: We had better start cranking up a charity operation.

So, with need not seen since the 1930's and an indifferent White House and Governor's Mansion, CACLV had to re-engineer itself to be relevant in the new world. And we better hustle, since the Thornburgh Administration's Department of Community Affairs had put us on probation, expecting us to make significant progress toward getting our act together in just a couple months.

We closed our neighborhood centers in Allentown, where I had gotten my start, and in Bethlehem's Marvine Village, the housing authority's largest project. We laid off seven of our 16 employees, including the wonderful woman who hired me – (I hate irony), and developed a completely new strategy. We would create a new safety net, with food pantries and soup kitchens and energy assistance (eventually we added homeless shelters to the list), so that the worse things got, the more we'd be needed. Additionally, we would take a partnership approach to these new initiatives, teaming with other groups for two reasons: One, because none of us had the money to go it alone anymore, and two, because we wanted allies the next time a president (or governor or anyone else, for that matter) proposed killing us.

It was a pretty raw strategy, brilliant in its practicality and almost sinister in its approach. We had already started the process of creating a regional food bank that we would call the "Lehigh Valley Food Bank." We did our first delivery, 10,000 pounds of industry-donated product distributed from the back of a rented truck to a dozen non-profits, in October, 1982.

Our probationary period had been extended from September 30 to December 31, at which time probation was lifted. We had survived, and were on a roll.

The block grant that was created in the compromise between congressional Democrats and the Reagan Administration was cut by 25 percent. However, because we had shut down much of what we had been doing, and were almost starting over, any funding we received felt like new money.

Then the Thornburgh Administration did something really right. They decided that communities should receive funding on a formula based on unemployment and poverty. It turns out that, when we were getting funding straight from the federal government, we were getting less than our fair share. The Thornburgh formula resulted in our funding being doubled! Because the realignment of funding was so radical, it was phased in over three years. And I had begun pursuing private contributions, something few Community Action Agencies were doing, including CACLV. As a result, we leveraged still more funding. As our agency grew and we added services and we raised our profile through a successful media strategy, we gained a louder voice and more power.

Chapter 4

I Hope This Book Gives You Hope

TWO 24-YEAR-OLDS (INCLUDING YOURS TRULY), BY THE GRACE OF GOD, INCREDIBLE LUCK OR WHATEVER YOU BELIEVE IN FIND THEMSELVES REBUILDING A NONPROFIT THAT, IN 1982, ANNOUNCED IT WOULD CLOSE. WE HAD A $500,000 BUDGET THAT YEAR. WE LAID OFF SEVEN OF OUR 16 EMPLOYEES.

We turned that around and, over the next 34 years, did the following:

We started the Lehigh Valley Food Bank, later changing the name to the Second Harvest Food Bank, which has supplied more than 140 million pounds of food since 1982 to a network of 200 nonprofits over six counties to provide food assistance to more than 60,000 people per month;

We created the Sixth Street Shelter and two long-term transitional facilities that have helped more than 4,000 families overcome crises, get on the right track and, hopefully, never need us again;

We weatherized more than 25,000 homes and repaired or replaced more than 1,000 furnaces;

We helped well over 30,000 households maintain utility service while sticking to a negotiated payment plan on their arrearages;

We helped a couple hundred businesses get started;

We lent over $7 million to almost 200 businesses;

We dramatically changed the complexion of homeownership, coaching more than 3,000 families through the process, almost 70 percent of whom are African-American or Latino, while 90 percent have incomes below 80 percent of the median;

We discovered and dogged the system to prosecute a massive mortgage fraud scheme that ripped off over 200 low-income, minority, inner-city homebuyers and put three creeps in jail (if the FBI wanted more, they could have nailed another dozen);

We trained hundreds of folks who are lower-income and/or of color in leadership skills and difference-making as board members of our five nonprofit corporations;

Our neighborhood revitalization efforts improved hundreds of residential and commercial property facades, rehabbed two dozen houses for resale, created several pocket parks and helped create a sizable skate park, planted more than 700 trees, street-scaped a whole city block, replaced 150 sidewalks, and installed scores of streetlights;

We have nagged every bank in the market and generated, in the process, easily $1 billion in housing, community and economic development commitments;

We affected many federal, state and local laws and ordinances, from budgets to minimum wage increases;

We organized and led the passage of two voter referenda that generated over $60 million in open space and municipal park funding;

Over those years, we expanded the organization's budget by a factor of 50 and its number of employees by a factor of 10, while acquiring and occupying more than $8 million worth of properties;

And we got awards from far and wide -- national awards, state awards and scads of local awards, awards from faith-based groups and business groups, from political groups and civic groups.

AND YOU CAN, TOO

Seriously. All you need to do is obsess, fight like hell, cajole, beg, threaten, manipulate and never let up. Well, OK, and you have to be cheap, angry, patient, impatient, persistent. Oh, and have vision. Understanding politics and economics helps. And believing you're right. That might be the most important one. Ready?

Chapter 5

The Starting Point

MAYBE YOU'RE A COLLEGE STUDENT YEARNING TO SAVE THE WORLD. You might be mid-career and sick of what you're doing. Or a person of faith who feels the institution isn't focused enough on what's important. How about an executive director who knows the nonprofit could be better if she pushed as hard as the people they serve deserved? Maybe you're adjunct at an elite university and can't find required reading worthy of your class. Maybe stories told by a brash punk about a brash punk's antics are of interest. Maybe you just want to know that the world could be better and there are people trying their best to make it so. Maybe you can actually join the cause. We'd welcome you.

But if you think this field is somehow easier than where your are, close this book, give it to someone who gets it, and get a job as an usher in a minor league baseball park. Or be a volunteer, or do it part-time.

This work should be an obsession. You should be burning with an intensity deep in your gut and searing your brain to make, in the words of the Old Testament prophet Amos, "justice flow like a river and righteousness like an ever-flowing stream."

And, if it is an obsession, what are the values that bring you to this point? Really, there is no more values-driven work than the struggle to resist all of the base forces of humankind – selfishness, xenophobia, hatred, ignorance, conceit, greed – in order to make the world a better place for those who have little hope without an army of sympathizers.

Are you willing to offend people? Break the rules? Go to jail? Is there a higher calling? What price are you willing to pay? Are you willing to miss your daughter's recital? Die? (OK, my wife would say I'm being overly dramatic.) Maybe. Maybe not.

And is your drive so intense that you can't compromise? That's the death knell for pursuit of the cause, and the reason why government can't get anything done anymore.

Chapter 6

Institutional Vehicles for Promoting Change

GOVERNMENT CAN AND SHOULD BE A VEHICLE FOR CHANGE. Certainly, we liberals see it that way. The problem is that this is a democracy (at least we try to be) and there is anything but a consensus on the role of government as a change agent. Plus, governments change and they often change all too quickly, so government as a change agent has serious limitations.

The for-profit sector is the best place to grow institutional vehicles to promote change thanks to minimal reporting requirements. They can earn their own money and pursue change unencumbered by politics. That is, essentially, the whole idea behind the concept of social entrepreneurship. Ben and Jerry's is one that does it particularly well. But there are too few that do.

That leaves the non-profit sector. Now, far too few in the nonprofit world have the the sophistication or even the kind of missionary zeal to see how important the change agent role is for a nonprofit. But how it collects resources, how it is governed, the culture that develops in an organization that, if done right, exists for the purpose of making a difference, becomes a perfect vehicle for being part of the fight to save the world.

This book, among other things, is a manual on how to use a nonprofit as an institutional vehicle for changing (read "saving") the world.

Chapter 7

Whatever You Call It, Do it

COALITION-BUILDING, COLLECTIVE IMPACT, ADVOCACY, LOBBYING, THREATENING THE BASTARDS, STANDING UP TO THOSE IN POWER, ANY AND ALL, NO MATTER WHAT YOU CALL IT, IT'S ALL PART OF BEING A CHANGE AGENT.

If you want to make the world a better place, you should be constantly identifying problems, innovating solutions, pulling in like-minded prospective allies, being noisy without looking goofy.

IF YOUR NONPROFIT ISN'T A CHANGE AGENT, YOU SIMPLY AREN'T DOING YOUR JOB.

Seriously.

If all were well in our world, the role of a nonprofit might arguably be to preserve the status quo. Of course, all is anything but well. Nonprofits exist, by and large, to make the world a better place, whether it is to feed hungry people, educate our children, protect our environment, provide a place of worship, heal the sick or tackle any number of other wrongs that need to be righted. I could run the best food bank around. But Congress could wipe out those gains and more in just a few minutes by how they vote on eligibility for school lunches or appropriations for the Supplemental Nutrition Assistance Program (or SNAP, the new name for Food Stamps).

Frankly, there should be a lot of former nonprofit executive directors out there, because there are far too many who aren't doing this part of their jobs. Only a tiny fraction of the nonprofits with which I have ever come into contact do advocacy, much less lobby for public policy improvements. If you don't see yourself as a change agent, you're in the wrong field. When it comes right down to it, if there is a single point of this wide-ranging rant, it is this one. The rest of this book is detail, how-to, stories, and justification for why, how, when you pursue the change agent agenda.

What change agents need is a values statement. Those values, if embraced properly, set the tone for how we will do what we do. It should set a tone that will create the culture you need to get the job done. And it ensures that most of us as colleagues can pretty confidently proceed in our work knowing exactly what we stand for. I am damned proud of this values statement. I call it our manifesto. You can find it in the appendix. It's all there: justice over charity; sacrifice, an obsession with "stewardship," honesty, the power of power. The board of directors softened some of my choices of words. For example, my phrase was, "We don't do anything for anyone." Instead, our board said it this way: "We give people the tools to solve their own problems, rather than solve those problems for them."

My hope is that, when this book has lost any appeal it might ever have had, people will say it moved dozens, maybe thousands, preferably every single nonprofit to do community problem-solving, advocacy, lobbying, and any other activity that will improve the lives of the folks next door.

Check out what we have been able to do over the years through our advocacy efforts.

HOUSING
Shelter, transitional housing and services for homeless people
- I served as a founding member of two nonprofits, one that created another shelter, transitional housing and single-room housing for people with disabilities while the other was the Lehigh Valley chapter of Habitat for Humanity.

- We organized and provided staff support for an affordable housing coalition for 25 years that ran the longest-running community-wide shelter census in the country, raised hundreds of thousands of dollars for the shelters from suburban municipalities, produced a public education video on homelessness, developed a coordinated, region-wide housing assistance network.

- We initiated and played a key role in passing a change in the 1983 Emergency Food and Shelter Program administered by the Federal Emergency Management Agency that made the program more responsive to the needs of people in crisis and the organizations struggling to serve them.

Affordable Housing
- The affordable housing coalition also created an affordable housing loan pool, convinced both counties we serve to raise mortgage- and deed-recording fees that have generated approximately $10 million for housing development (that started with convincing the legislature to pass a law authorizing counties to raise such levies), created a down payment and closing cost assistance program that financed more than 1,000 first-time home purchases.

- Led a campaign to create an apartment licensing program in Allentown to increase code enforcement and crack down on slum landlords and cite residents for "disruptive behavior" that diminishes the quality of life for the neighbors.

- Helped create and operate a community land trust that has offered two dozen rehabbed or newly-constructed homes for sale to first-time homebuyers.

- Created a single, community-wide homeownership counseling campaign that has literally changed the complexion of homebuyers in our market.

- Fought predatory lending, bringing a massive mortgage fraud conspiracy to the attention of federal prosecutors that resulted in three co-conspirators going to prison and helping change laws at the state and federal level; convinced both county court systems to create a "diversion court" to protect homeowners from foreclosure.

- Played a key role in getting approval for Easton's HOPE VI redevelopment of its decades-old Delaware Terrace project.

COMMUNITY REINVESTMENT

- Negotiated community reinvestment commitments from banks during nine acquisitions/mergers totaling well over $700 million in loans, investments and services.

- Generated more than $5 million in corporate grants for comprehensive neighborhood redevelopment projects in the cities of Allentown, Bethlehem and Easton.

MISCELLANEOUS CAMPAIGNS

- Organized voter referenda to raise more than $65 million for open space preservation and municipal parks.

- Developed a novel health care program for uninsured families while a head-of-household was unemployed.

- Played an important role in passing a variety of legislation, including raising the minimum wage, creating Pennsylvania's unique State Food Purchase Program and its one-of-a-kind Homeowners' Emergency Mortgage Assistance Program.

- Created a smart growth advocacy organization.

- Countless other public policy campaigns, including fighting federal and state budget cuts.

I am proud of what we have accomplished. I am disappointed where we failed. But we tried, and we keep trying. Now let's get into some nuts-and-bolts.

We've gotten just about every award given out here in the Lehigh Valley, and even a few well beyond (for example, CACLV has an award from the National Community Reinvestment Coalition that was handed to me by the Reverend Jesse Jackson). I have appreciated and am quite proud of every one of those awards. While the agency's awards are proudly displayed in our main offices, the personal awards I've received are in a box under the table in my office. I can't display them – it feels too self-promoting.

Chapter 8

Community Action Agencies

YOU'VE PROBABLY HEARD OF THE "WAR ON POVERTY," BUT YOU MAY NOT KNOW VERY MUCH ABOUT THE ORGANIZATIONS CONCEIVED AS THE LOCAL VEHICLES FOR DELIVERING THE WAR ON POVERTY IN YOUR COMMUNITY.

They are called Community Action Agencies. Prior to Lyndon Johnson's War on Poverty, the federal government played a minimal role in fighting poverty in America. There were subsidized housing projects, Social Security and Aid to Dependent Children, but not much else. Poverty was seen as a local issue. However, the likelihood of politicians raising taxes on the folks on one side of the tracks in order to assist those on the other side of the tracks was something close to zip. Consequently, little was done. Johnson's War on Poverty changed all of that.

He proposed establishing a network of organizations nationwide that would organize poor people to fight the forces that held people back, in other words, obstacles to self-sufficiency. Local communities would have to take formal action in support of the establishment of what they then called, "Community Action Programs." Funding would come straight from the federal government, taking many of the rednecks, thugs, reactionaries and even reasonable opponents at the local level out of the equation. With money straight from the feds, they could take steps unimpaired by the resistance that had always prevented the local community from doing the right thing in the first place.

A key provision of the CAP model was insisting that CAA's organize poor people and train them to find their collective voice to, effectively, challenge city hall.

Representatives of those organized groups would then serve on the board of directors of the CAA.

There is an age-old argument about whether economic gains stem from political power or political power comes from economic gains. The War on Poverty sided with the former. But those with political power were not going to give up either that power or their financial resources even if they considered themselves liberals and supporters of the cause. Board meetings, including those overseeing the CAA here in the Lehigh Valley, became contentious and fraught with hostility. Some, including here, were almost comical in their dysfunction.

And, yet, most anti-poverty programs developed in those early years had to go through the CAA in order to be approved by the feds. It put many CAA's in a position of power. Legal services on civil matters, Head Start, family planning, job training and other services were often started and operated by CAA's. Some CAA's continued to operate these programs and became massive organizations, some with budgets today in excess of $100 million. Some, like ours, spun some or all of those programs off to become separate corporate entities. In a lot of communities, especially in rural places, the CAA is just about all they've got.

Today, there are more than 1,000 CAA's. Some are sophisticated, well-run, entrepreneurial and responsive. Others, not so much. Unfortunately, we always seem to have the worst CAA's in the most strategically important congressional districts. When a younger Barack Obama was organizing in Chicago, for example, he came to dislike the CAA. Joe Biden wasn't a fan of his in Delaware. As president, Obama offered up the CAA funding as a sacrificial lamb, proposing to cut our funding in half.

CAA's are perfect for the use of the kinds of tactics and strategies promoted in this text. Unfortunately, many CAA's have leadership that doesn't get the empowerment agenda, running largely agencies that have that disempowering human services agenda, administering government contracts that make it difficult to do advocacy. We are all paying a price for that approach.

Photograph courtesy of Keenan-Nagle Advertising, Inc.

Section II

Help, They Need Somebody

Chapter 9

Nonprofits and Their Boards of Directors

A NONPROFIT ORGANIZATION CAN BE A VERY EFFECTIVE VEHICLE FOR TRYING TO CHANGE THE WORLD. The tax exemption that nonprofits can get from the Internal Revenue Service, as defined in the Internal Revenue Code, means they don't have to pay many of the taxes paid by individuals or for-profit entities. Perhaps more importantly, individuals and corporations can get a tax deduction for their contributions to your cause. There are some things you need to know, though.

You probably know this, but it bears repeating: The board of directors is where the responsibility, legal liability, and, yes, power reside in a nonprofit. Too many executive directors (probably, in particular, those who call themselves "president and CEO") act otherwise.

There should be a strong commitment, then, from the board in all of its endeavors. That commitment should take on many forms, to wit:

- They need to attend, at the least, half of the meetings, as well as committee meetings, and actively share their perspectives;
- They should read the materials provided and demand more, if necessary, to conduct business effectively;
- If at all possible, they should donate;
- They should promote the organization's work in the community.

It's a challenge getting that standard met.

NOBODY IS IN CHARGE; EVERYBODY IS IN CHARGE
Having said all of that, no single board member, including the president or chair, whatever your nonprofit calls them, is the executive director's supervisor. It is the top volunteer who leads the board collectively in supervising the top staffer. If the board defers that responsibility, that can be dangerous. I don't even like executive committees and have done all I can to disempower mine: They have a tendency to become ruling juntas, letting the rest of the board off the hook or consolidating power in a way that locks many out of the process and makes them little more than the proverbial "rubber stamp." The result is that too few directors own responsibility for the organization.

Unless there are no or very limited paid staff, the board of directors' role in a well-established and managed organization is limited. Technically, those limits are up to the board, but I think there is relative consensus that the board has the following primary responsibilities:

- Hire, fire and evaluate the top staff person
- Fiduciary oversight
- Strategic planning.

POPULATING YOUR BOARD OF DIRECTORS
Let's begin as if you are creating a new organization and starting from scratch on establishing a board of directors. There are two models with catchy phrases for what to look for in a board of directors.

Workers, Wealth and Wisdom
Wouldn't it be nice? You get the workers who will hustle to get logistics done, you get the people with money to fund it and you get the wisdom to make good, consensus judgments. Baloney. You never know if any of these types of people will turn out to be what you expected. But it's a good way to look at what you need.

Give, Get or Get Out
I guess advocates of this trite expression are not interested in poor people having a say in the decisions that affect their lives. Just as significant an objection as that

one is that it places far too much priority on fundraising. You need lawyers (they are notorious for not giving), you need accountants (they, too, have a reputation for wanting to keep the money they count), you need people with expertise in the problems you want to solve, you want diversity, not just demographic but geographic and ideological, too.

Among the fundraising crowd, it is argued that every board member should be invested enough to make a financial contribution. Some of my peers argue that donors, including foundations, often require it. However, in all the years (35 of them) I've been raising money I think I have only had one or two prominent funders make that clear.

In my early twenties, I was recruited to serve on the board of one of the Planned Parenthood affiliates in our region. This organization put the full-court press on its board to give or get. I had nothing, no money. I simply could not afford to give. Plus, it was early in my career and I knew very few people who were particularly philanthropic. I couldn't give, I couldn't get and I felt so useless I would have gotten out. They wouldn't hear of it. But it stuck with me. I won't do that to my board members.

HERE'S THE CLOSEST I CAN COME TO A FORMULA

You need a lawyer and at least two or three strong financial minds. You need well-known people with unassailable reputations and, preferably, friends who have money to give away. You need three to five people who are experts in the field you are in. For example, if you are running a shelter for stray cats and dogs, you'll need a veterinarian, maybe an obedience trainer, and maybe someone who works for the county's "dog catcher." Or, if you are running a music school for low-income kids, you'll need a musician (preferably one who came from a poor family), a school music teacher, the owner of a store that sells instruments and sheet music. If you're rehabbing and reselling houses, you'll need a banker who knows mortgage lending, another banker who knows how to do commercial lending for real estate development, a builder, someone who sells real estate (try to find one who doesn't routinely violate fair housing laws), a contractor who doesn't need or want the work (to avoid that pesky conflict of interest problem), maybe an architect.

Of course, you can get people who cover more than one of the traits you are seeking in order to keep the size of the board down. Some argue that smaller boards are more desirable – they can be more agile and both easier and cheaper to manage. On the other hand, larger boards (ours is 24 directors) can cover more ground, know more people, have greater access to funding sources, represent more interests.

Diversity is a good thing on a board of directors. Diversity comes in many forms. First, of course, folks think that means demographic diversity. Yes, it means people of color. It also means old folks and young folks. It means geographic diversity. It means gender diversity.

And it means opinion diversity. Too many nonprofits are listening to themselves. To be sure, you want stalwarts on the board who get the cause, the context in which the cause was born and are even dug in on how to serve. But you also need people who, while still believers, dance to a different tune. Arguments are good for the organization. They force you to look at all sides, strengthen your argument in the face of disagreement or even resistance.

Perhaps most importantly, you need at least a few people who come from the population you are serving.

"A VOICE IN THE DECISIONS THAT AFFECT THEIR LIVES"
This phrase, in my opinion, is the most important part of our mission statement. Here is how I would put the point: Our society is far more threatened when poverty and deprivation lead to apathy and dependence than when it leads to anger and activism.

CHALLENGE, SCRUTINIZE AND QUESTION
The relationship between the board and the executive director should be supportive enough to get things done but challenging enough to make sure that the organization is the best it can be. I tell my board not to trust me. They can, but they shouldn't. They should not accept everything the staff says without question. The relationship between the executive director and the board should not be cozy. There should be term limits. The environment in a board meeting

should be professional, but discerning. I love being asked questions – it suggests the board cares and is inquisitive. When new directors ask questions, just about everyone else on the board is thankful. The longer one is on the board, the more they think they should know and the less they will allow their lack of knowledge to be apparent. They are usually relieved that an uninformed rookie asked the question.

THE DUTY OF LOYALTY AND TRUST
Few are aware of this concept. Board members are expected to work to make the organization as strong and consequential as possible. Disagreements should be kept within the family. Once a vote is taken, even those on the opposing side have an obligation to embrace the outcome. If a director, for whatever reason, can't do that, the director should not publicly voice that discontent; instead, the director should resign. Organizational disagreements should be kept within the family.

Internal dissent is, in my view, good for the organization if the volunteer leadership is effective at managing the debate. Boards should have a diversity of perspective that, if robust, can lead to better decision-making.

Unfortunately, few boards do manage that debate well. Unlike for-profit corporate boards, on which directors are paid and, therefore, more likely to have a dog in the fight, few directors are willing to have the battles that can lead to better decisions.

We were leading a campaign to strengthen code enforcement in Allentown. It was a good fight; details can be found elsewhere in these pages.

Neighborhood activists, most of whom were homeowners, wanted a provision to deal with so-called "disruptive tenants," those who make life difficult, if not unbearable, in dense urban neighborhoods. If a tenant was cited three times by the city in a 12-month period, the landlord would be obligated to evict. Disruptive behavior is considered the types of things we once called "disturbing the peace." It wasn't my idea but I liked it.

An activist for Latino causes objected, calling it "racist." The activist was on CACLV's board of directors. Uh oh. Looks like one of those situations where a domestic quarrel won't be staying within the family.

I guess he was saying that Latinos are loud and that their noisiness should be tolerated because they are Latino. Geez. Sounds like a stereotype.

Here's a Lehigh Valley reality: This is a very segregated community. The likelihood of a Latino living next to another Latino is very high. Don't they, too, have a right to their kids getting a good night's sleep on a school night?

This isn't a race issue, and it's not a class issue. It's an asshole issue – nobody wants to live next to an asshole.

So, this board member makes his point in a committee meeting of the board. I had had enough. He might as well be calling me a racist. I walked out of the meeting, went straight to my phone and called the president of the board.

I said, "I have had it with this guy. If I'm a racist, fire me. If I'm not, he has to go." I told her I would resign if he was not removed, then went home.

I waited. I gave her a deadline. Waited some more. Nothing.

This board of directors was apparently willing to lose their long-time executive director who helped save the agency, expanded its budget by a factor of more than ten at that point, and attracted extensive press coverage and a variety of awards because nobody had the guts to confront a rogue board member (my view, of course).

I was broken. I could not believe the situation. I cut the grass, ignored my phone messages.

They delivered flowers and balloons. I finally backed off, swallowing more pride than even I thought I had.

But I have been resentful all these years. It was one of the darkest moments of my career.

In hindsight, I put my own interests, maybe even my own ego, ahead of the very real alienation so many people of color experience in our society. My attitude was, hey, you've got the most sympathetic white boy on the planet fighting for the cause, how dare you call my work racist?

I was personally offended and deeply hurt that a board member would view a proposal that I supported as racist and by implication was insinuating that I myself—and to this day I think he was just plain wrong. In hindsight, however, I realize that, whether he was right or wrong, if he truly believed what he was saying, then making his point as forcefully as he could within the confines of the boardroom was not only his right but his obligation as a board member, and I should have been tough enough to hear his opinion, disagree with it as eloquently as I could, and move on.

While I certainly could have reacted more gracefully, that episode did make it painfully clear to me that board members will rarely hang in there for an internal fight. In fact, when things get even a little contentious, uncomfortable volunteers will usually just quit, denying the organization an important element in good decision-making. So, either carefully vet board prospects or do an effective job of training board members to participate.

BOARDS ARE EXPENSIVE; USE THEM WISELY
At CACLV, we have five separate nonprofitss, which means five separate charters, five separate profit/loss statements, five balance sheets, five audits and, yes, five separate boards of directors, each of which has committees. We also have two advisory boards, four steering committees, and a bunch of ad hoc groups. We don't think about these groups as cost centers but we probably should. Staff support for each includes meeting notices, minutes and/or notes for the record, reports, financial documentation, staff time to plan and coordinate and more.

We wrote, for lack of a better word, a manual on how we expect staff to support that vast volunteer network that keeps us honest and making good decisions.

STEAL THIS MANUAL
We called it "A Manual on the Care and Feeding of CACLV's Volunteer Boards, Steering Committees and Advisory Boards." (One of our most active board members was offended by the name, calling it "condescending," so we gave it a new name. But I like it and will use it here.)

The entire manual can be found in the appendices. For those like me who are too hyper to read it, following are the key points.

PROVIDING STAFF SUPPORT FOR THE BOARD OF DIRECTORS
Staff members serve as resources for a nonprofits's volunteer board and its committees; they are not members of the board and they do not have a vote in decision-making. Staff will offer assistance as needed or requested. Usually, staff will record minutes or notes of a meeting. Room reservations, refreshments, and any other considerations for the meeting space are staff responsibilities. Staff is also charged with developing agendas, raising issues, and providing background for deliberations. At all times, staff will defer to the directors and implement the decisions of the governing entity.

Prior to every meeting of a board or committee, staff should consult with the presiding officer regarding the agenda, information needed for decision-making, and the expectations of the meeting. Staff, in consultation with the presiding officer, should compose motions for the board's actions.

Staff should be in touch with board members as issues arise. Because decision-making is dependent on having complete factual information, staff members can assist board members by discussing all aspects of the issues with the presiding officer and/or other board members. While staff should be careful to avoid looking manipulative, they should identify and work with directors who will support staff recommendations and are willing to advance that cause. Get it? Use your allies. Let them know what's coming and how you need their help.

Staff does not chair meetings nor do they dominate discussion; the board meeting is a meeting of the volunteers, not the staff. Ideally, staff "speak when spoken to" or report as requested by the board except for the top staff person attending the meeting. Most staff should not sit at the board table unless invited to do so. Staff members need to remember that boards make decisions about budgets, programs, and personnel matters; they need to respect the board's role and be extremely cautious in their interactions with the directors. Open defiance is never acceptable.

MEETINGS ARE THE OFFICIAL BUSINESS OF THE ORGANIZATION; DO THEM RIGHT
It is important for the smooth functioning of a board of directors that the directors get timely information, preferably three or more days prior to a meeting.

The following should be included in those board packets: a meeting notice and agenda for the upcoming meeting; minutes of the board's most recent previous meeting; anticipated or proposed action items, meaning motions; fiscal reports; background information for any discussion or action item; and reports. I hate to be so anal, but these documents should have a consistent "look" that includes keeping the documents in the same order, printing them in the same font, and formatting them in the same way. That might sound pretty neurotic, but the better the rhythm of this process, the more effective the board will be.

MINUTES ARE THE OFFICIAL RECORD OF THE CORPORATION; DO THEM RIGHT, TOO
Minutes are the record of the proceedings of the board; every corporate board is required to keep minutes. Although staff may prepare the minutes, the secretary of the board is responsible for the minutes and indicates that responsibility by signing an "official" document.

Minutes should really only record the business that was conducted at the meeting; they are not a blow-by-blow, he-said-she-said account of every aspect of the meeting.

In general, minutes should include:

- the name of the organization and the date and time the board met (and adjourned);

- attendance of board members, staff, and guests and a list of the board members who were excused or absent;
- the name of the person who presided;
- the approval of the previous meeting's minutes (by board vote);
- a brief description of board, staff, or committee reports that were presented;
- all motions, formatted for easy reference, and the outcome of the vote;
- the secretary should sign all minutes to indicate approval.

The minutes should indicate that a motion was made and seconded and the fact that the motion was approved or disapproved. Although it is not required that the names of the person who made the motion and the person who seconded the motion be recorded, it is a courtesy to note their involvement in the action. The inclusion of a brief background on a motion is helpful so that, in the future, it will be clear why the board took this action.

IT'S EASIER TO SEEK FORGIVENESS THAN PERMISSION

Maybe. But you can't rely on that as a strategy. And a relationship based on the executive director trying to get away with things can't be healthy.

We bought a straight truck for our regional food bank from a locally-owned dealer. The owner had a reputation for his philanthropy, mostly through what used to be called the Boys Club. He lived across the cornfield from me when I was growing up; my older brother dated his eldest daughter and my younger brother dated his younger daughter briefly. It's a small world here in the Lehigh Valley.

Despite his assurances, the truck wasn't what we needed. We figured that out on the first delivery. So, I tried to get him to take it back. Couldn't get a return phone call. His eldest daughter, who I liked, wasn't getting me anywhere either. I tried and tried to get some sort of resolution, to no avail. I'm generally a pretty angry guy. I'm so sick of injustice that the slightest slight fires me up.

I probably didn't have any legal standing. But I thought I had something better: moral authority.

Time for a fight. My plan was to take his truck to his dealership and block the entrance to the property. I would call the police ahead of time and also alert the media. I figured he might respond to a high, inside fastball. That's what we call "reputational risk." Nobody wants to be embarrassed publicly, especially not a retail business. And screwing the Food Bank would be one serious embarrassment. I was willing to face the consequences, maybe even get arrested; it would be well worth those consequences.

But I made a tactical error. I asked the board for permission to do it. The weenies voted no. We ended up trading it in to another truck dealership.

Damn it. I learned a lesson.

BYLAWS

I'm not going to get into bylaws in any depth but I would argue for minimalist bylaws. For example, our bylaws identify as few standing committees as possible so that the bylaws don't have to be changed each time a committee is created or killed. Be sure to have a strong conflict of interest provision and indicate where the residual resources of the organization will go if it is shut down.

And set term limits. This is one of my biggest beefs with nonprofit boards of directors. It is difficult to challenge an executive director effectively if there are long-term relationships between the board and top staff. Also, new ideas, new ways of looking at things, new ways of doing things are difficult to conjure if new blood isn't coursing through the veins of the organization.

I once gave up my coveted seat on the board of directors of a national organization because the board's nominating committee penned me in for another three-year term. They didn't even ask. Several directors had been on the board since its founding twenty

GETTING ARRESTED FOR THE CAUSE

So, I've had my share of run-ins with the law. I have done the calculation many times. How do you balance the consequences with the expected or hoped-for outcome (fun, political, revenge, etc.)? MLK did it and Gandhi did, too, both for the cause of justice. I'm willing but for the right impact. Stealing Christmas trees doesn't make the grade.

But a homeless, young mother with her toddler illegally locked out of an illegal boarding room does.

A local gadfly posted a video online about this young mom. It moved me. OK, it pissed me off.

The mom was in her early twenties, the child not even two. She was living in a boarding house, what we call a single-room occupancy, or SRO (which, conveniently, also stands for "standing room only"). However, the building was such a dump that the city of Allentown had tagged it as unfit for human habitation. So, the owner of this travesty, which illustrated plenty of the state of affairs here, was renting the building out illegally. The city knew that, and did nothing about it because the mayor didn't want to create more homelessness.

According to the video, the landlord locked the young family out of the room and building. She did it illegally; no eviction notice, no due process. All they had was, literally, the clothes they were wearing. And it was winter. So I called the landlord. I left a message on her voicemail. I told her who I was. I told her she had until 4 PM the next day to let the young mom in. If she didn't, I would break in.

Early afternoon came around the next day and I got no call. I called the chief of police years earlier. There were no term limits and the prospect of whether I would serve another term wasn't even in question on the part of the CEO or the nominating committee. Everyone was stunned when I declined the additional term. Nice folks, good work, sorry I'm no longer on the board, but I've got principles, you know.

HOW DO YOU TELL YOUR BOARD, POLITELY, TO STAY THE HELL OUT OF YOUR BUSINESS?

You don't. But there are limits to board member "meddling," as long as you agree on what meddling is. Generally, board members should want to know enough about what is going on in the organization to avoid being embarrassed by its weaknesses. Directors' and officers' liability insurance is a must – it will protect board members from stupid mistakes but not wantonly stupid mistakes. Directors should stay out of the daily operations, let the staff do the hiring (although I think it wise to involve directors in key decisions). For example, it makes sense for the board treasurer to participate in hiring the fiscal director. Once a board is overly engaged or overly disengaged, it will take a while to change that culture.

and explained the situation. "Roger, at 4 this afternoon, I'm going to break in. You're welcome to arrest me." He chuckled and thanked me for the courtesy call.

Next was my call to the news media.

At 4 PM, with one of the coolest, most progressive lawyers in this community along for protection, I showed up at the door of the dump passing as a home for some pretty unfortunate souls. The local independent television news folks showed up. So did a reporter from the local newspaper. I had a crow bar. It didn't do the trick. So I sent one of my cohorts to get a Sawzall. While we waited, a regular guy, possibly a neighborhood resident, maybe an employee of the slum landlord, happens along. He stops amid the small crowd, and asks what's up. I told him we were trying to break into the building. He says, "Oh. Well, I have a key!"

You have got to be kidding me.

He opens the door. The reporter from the daily paper, irritated that I wasn't going to be arrested, leaves. He later told me that my stunt was the story and when I didn't get arrested, there wasn't a story.

The real story was the horrible housing conditions poor people had to endure. The city's inability to be vigilant in enforcing the various laws and the rules and regulations they spawned was another part of the story. Designed to correct these conditions and protect the tenants from threats to their health and safety, here was evidence that all was still not well in our fair city.

We walk in. We help her get her things. She leaves, heading for the home of a friend. Another opportunity to use civil disobedience to make a point lost. Damn it. Our local, independent television news station covered it anyway, so did a key local blogger, so it wasn't a total loss.

Chapter 10

So, You're Clean? Check Again

I'M NOT SURE WE SHOULD PUT THESE UNDER THE REPORTER TEST, BUT THEY SURE FIT UNDER "RIGHT VERSUS WRONG" WHEN IT COMES TO RUNNING AN EFFECTIVE CAMPAIGN TO SAVE YOUR WORLD.

DIVERSITY
Change agents shouldn't have any exposure to attack from someone who can legitimately point out that we don't walk the talk. Actually, back up. Talk about race. This country has a race problem; denying it is, essentially, racist. So, push the issue. But you better walk like that duck. You should be diverse all through the organization, from the rank and file, up through the management ranks and all the way to the top, the board of directors. Don't let anyone beat you on this issue.

ADMINISTRATIVE COSTS
We have a saying: "There's cheap. Then there's CACLV cheap." Our agency has consistently kept its administrative costs under 10 percent of our budget. That's outstanding. Anything under 15 percent is pretty damn good. Donors, taxpayers, the public at-large all deserve responsible overhead expenses. We are obsessed with stewardship. You should be, too.

CONTRACT COMPLIANCE
The radicals on the right will never be satisfied. But we have a duty to be in compliance with all our contractual obligations. The problem is that, because those on the right are fundamentally and viscerally opposed to just about all we

do, they are not only cutting our funding but are making it harder and harder to meet those obligations. The paperwork keeps getting more demanding while our resources are shrinking. Something has to give. It can't be contract compliance.

WAGES AND OTHER EMPLOYMENT-RELATED PRINCIPLES

Don't be caught being a hypocrite. If we believe the minimum wage should be increased, shouldn't we increase our wages to the level we are seeking? I had planned on raising the wages of our lowest-paid employees when we were successful at changing the law. My employees, God bless them, pointed out how wrong that was. They were right. We raised the wages of the few people who were under $10.10 to get our own lowest wages up to what we were supporting.

We pushed a law years ago that required employers that cut more than 200 jobs to give their workers a 30-day notice of the lay-offs. We don't have 200 employees (it's more like 100) but we stand by our own principles, so when we do a rare lay-off we give those affected at least 30 days.

The same thing goes for health benefits for our employees. It's only right that we offer good, affordable benefits, as difficult as it may be.

TOO SMALL TO SUCCEED

If you are thinking about starting a new nonprofit, think twice … or take your time in determining not to do it. There is widespread agreement that there are too many in our area and, except in fairly remote rural areas, probably in yours, too. There is broad consensus that we should consolidate. My advice is that you create a program and shop it around to existing nonprofits, and convince them to add it to their portfolio and hire you to run it.

Remember, small nonprofits struggle to keep up with administrative demands due to severely restricted capacity. And, inevitably, someone is getting paid too much to answer phones or too little to raise money or manage the organization.

CONFLICT OF INTEREST

This issue is particularly dangerous. The landscape is littered with new rules, new standards, new expectations, all of which evolve. It might be a reporter who's on to something. It might be another nonprofit looking for a way to weaken you. It might be a fellow board member who has been looking for a way to discredit you. There is a very simple test: Are you doing this work for you or for someone else? Are you sacrificing or accumulating? Giving or taking?

If you are involved with a nonprofit, the bylaws should address conflicts of interest. I'm not sure anyone has written the perfect template for your bylaws that will protect you and all others involved from engaging in behavior that serves competing interests. Sometimes your funding sources will have a model template. But do not rest. Put this book down and go write yourself a note reminding you to get on this – now!

Chapter 11

Fundraising

DO IT, FOR CRYING OUT LOUD. IT'S REALLY VERY SIMPLE: JUST ASK PEOPLE FOR MONEY.

OK, sorry for being flip, but seriously, it really is just a matter of asking. Get used to getting "no" for an answer. If your self-esteem can handle rejection, you're well on your way to being a fine fundraiser. So, my challenge now is to help the reader learn how to minimize those hits to your self-esteem.

YOUR ORGANIZATION MUST BE WELL-RUN
Step one is having a product that has value in your community. Be sure you have mastered the things in this book that you need to do to have a relatively flawless organization. People won't give to a shitty organization even if the cause is righteous. While some folks might be able to sell a refrigerator to the proverbial Eskimo, it sure helps if the fridge works.

PROSPECTIVE DONORS NEED TO UNDERSTAND THE CAUSE
This starts with a well-documented assessment of the need. Once you think you have that, find some natural opponents or at least indifferent people and run your case past them. They will help you refine the case and maybe even embrace the cause.

Every cause has its complexity, its warts, its subtleties. A constituency that is knowledgeable about a need is an important starting point. Educating the community is an essential element to any change agent's strategy. Pay careful attention to the chapter that explains how to effectively use the media. Also, make sure you refine The Message – that's in here, too.

KNOW WHO YOUR PROSPECTIVE SUPPORTERS MIGHT BE
By now you may have gotten used to, maybe even comfortable with, my crudeness. So, here's another crude point: Know who sleeps with whom. I mean that both figuratively and literally. Women, let's be honest, care more about others than we stupid men do. If you think the CEO of a local company might be able to give a lot but you can't get to him, get to his wife. If the CEO is a woman, you're in even better shape.

This is really all about relationships. Talk to people. Use your best charm and sales skills.

Think about natural constituencies of your cause. If your issue is open space preservation, for example, identify the folks who live in big houses across from farms that are vulnerable to the financial appeal a developer can make to that hard-working but still poor farmer. When we were organizing a voter referendum to raise funds for open space preservation the first group's endorsement I pursued was the homebuilders'. I said, "Chuck, there's an old saying: If you're not at the table, you're probably on the menu. Don't you want to be at the table?" They signed on.

If your issue is urban revitalization, get to the banks (the federal Community Reinvestment Act is a powerful tool to give bankers an incentive to support saving urban neighborhoods) or existing businesses in the struggling neighborhood.

If your cause is children, ask any mom, children's store or pediatrician (actually, doctors are notoriously lousy givers). You get the picture.

When you go to a hospital or other nonprofit, look at the plaques that name the donors who helped ay for the building you're in. Study the lists of board members of other like-minded nonprofits.

DON'T WASTE YOUR TIME ON EVENTS

When Bill Cosby announced the Hands Across America event during the Super Bowl, I went into panic mode. The crazy-assed idea was that Americans would hold hands, creating a human chain that would literally go from New York to Los Angeles. The event was scheduled for May 25, 1986, and, as the leading advocate on the issue of hunger and homelessness in the Lehigh Valley, I was instantly petrified by the challenge of connecting northwest New Jersey with Reading, Pennsylvania. I imagined being responsible for the failure of the event. I could just picture Tom Brokaw: "Good evening, the much ballyhooed hand-holding event intended to form a human chain of Americans concerned about their homeless citizens was a huge success today, except for the failure of one lone community in Pennsylvania. Alan Jennings of the Community Action Committee of the Lehigh Valley, charged with organizing that community, was not available for comment today."

I did the math: With the average wingspan of an adult being, maybe, five feet and the distance between the two points being about 57 miles, I was in deep trouble.

I wondered how I would motivate thousands of people to join the line. I decided I would mobilize the Baby Boomers, that generation that was all about social consciousness, by reuniting three popular bands from the 1960's that came out of the Lehigh Valley. Those who joined the line would get into the show for free. All others paid $12.

I started with the easy one, The Shillings (my brother's band). While not a national name, they had had a song that hit Number One in the New England market in the mid-Sixties. Mark was still getting his kicks playing in a band in Salem, Oregon. Tom Ross, the other front man, had died, so Mark and the drummer were the only two from the early days who played but the two guys they recruited to stand in were outstanding.

Then I approached Jay and the Techniques, who came out of Allentown. They were the first integrated pop band to score a Top Ten hit. Their records, "Apples Peaches Pumpkin Pie" and "Keep the Ball Rolling," sold millions. They were given their gold record for "Keep the Ball Rolling" on the Ed Sullivan Show on New Year's Eve in 1967.

I asked Jay Sands, a household name in the region from his days as one of the DJs at the top AM pop radio station, how to find someone from the band. He told me he had heard that John Walsh was tending bar at an iconic restaurant in Allentown called The Village Inn that has since closed. John played trumpet.

I walked in, plunked myself at the bar. One guy is behind the bar. "You John Walsh?"

"Yes."

"Still playing the horn?"

He pauses. "Not really."

"Want to?"

He stops.

"Want to get the band back together?" I felt like one of the Blues Brothers.

"No, no. That isn't going to happen."

I told him what I was trying to do. He was in.

"I can get to Jay." I'll get back to you.

Jay was in! So was George "Lucky" Lloyd, the other vocalist. In fact, they all agreed. We had a gig! Jay, who was a perfectionist, worried that some of the original guys had not kept their instrumental skills up. In fact, when they recorded their big hits, the only guy from the actual band in the studio was Jay. The others were session musicians put together by Mercury Records. The back-up vocalists, interestingly enough, were Melba Moore and Nickolas Ashford and his wife, Valerie Simpson. Yes, THAT Ashford and Simpson!

The original group, besides Jay, Lucky and John, were Ron Goosley, the saxophonist, and Chuck Crowl, the bassist, both of whom still lived in the area, Karl Lippowitsch, the drummer, who lived in Cincinnati, and Danny Dancho, the guitarist, who was in Mesa, Arizona. To get the most of the big sound they originally created, Jay filled in some serious local talent. At show-time there were 13 musicians on stage. In preparing for their return to the stage, Jay got the local guys together for several hours of serious rehearsal every Saturday afternoon for three months. Man, I was in my element, attending almost every rehearsal, in awe of what I was watching. They put together a show that was worthy of a Sixties-era variety show. They had songs planned that were hits for The Temptations, The Four Tops, Smoky Robinson and The Miracles, Otis Redding and others.

I also pursued The Cyrkle. They, too, had two big hits – "Red Rubber Ball" and "Turn Down Day." Four fellow students from Lafayette College in Easton, Pennsylvania, they had warmed up for the Beatles on their 1966 tour. The problem was that the two front men, Don Dannemann and the late Tom Dawes, had not spoken since the acrimonious end of the band almost 20 years earlier, not long after the tour with The Beatles. (On the day of the show, I listened to Don tell about being virtual hostages with the four lads, holed up in hotel rooms playing poker.)

The drummer for the Shillings, Hub Willson, told me he had seen one of those "Where Are They Now"-type pieces in Rolling Stone that reported on the activities of the guys who had made up The Cyrkle. Both Dannemann and Dawes were in New York, running competing businesses writing songs for commercials. Between them they had done "The Uncola Song" for 7 Up, "Stroh's is Spoken Here" and a bunch of others that would be recognizable to those of us who were around in 1986.

I called Dannemann and actually got him on the phone. "No way." I persisted. "We haven't spoken in 20 years." I persisted. "OK, if you can get Tom to do it, I will do it."

I called Dawes. "Sure!"

I called Dannemann. He said, "Good luck getting Marty and Earl." Marty Freed, the drummer, was an attorney in the Detroit area. Earl Pickens, the keyboard player, was a surgeon in Gainesville, Florida. Both readily agreed. Because they only had one day to prepare, they agreed to do just four songs. No problem, as long as "Red Rubber Ball" and "Turn Down Day" were among them. I arranged for them to meet in a music studio in New York where they would have that single day to prepare. I felt like I had pulled off a minor miracle.

I recruited Jay Sands to emcee the show. The radio station promoted the event. We had billboards all over the region promoting it. There was a full-page story in the local paper. We got a $3,500 sponsorship from the local Coca-Cola Bottling Company. About 1,500 people attended. The show was top notch.

We made $3,500. That's right. One phone call might have raised the same amount as all that work did. Additional collateral damage was that I struggled for weeks following the show, wondering what I could do for an encore after that triumphant event.

A few years ago, my board of directors suggested that we turn our Annual Meeting into a fun event, maybe even a fundraiser. Our Annual Meeting is usually a luncheon, a chance to show off our results for the year in front of 200 or more of our friends and allies and meet our obligation to have an annual meeting under our bylaws. It usually raises a small amount of money even though fundraising isn't the main purpose of the event.

So, we went back to Jay Proctor. This time we went out and got a bunch of corporate ads for a printed program and two prime sponsors totaling more than $35,000. It was a great evening, bank CEO's dancing right along with the poor folks on our board. We netted less than $15,000.

So, don't do events. They can be helpful as "friend-raisers" if you have dedicated volunteers and some events, if done right, can take off. But events, by and large, are not going to get you a good return on investment.

FINDING THE (MANY) NEEDLES IN THE HAYSTACK
So you have your product, it's well-run, you have the nerve to ask and the self-esteem needed to survive being rejected. Now you need prospects.

Start with the companies in your area. Find out their process for giving away money. Establish a relationship with the community relations staff that is who are responsible for philanthropy. Invite them to tour your operation.

Direct mail is a useful tool.

These days you can be downright surgical in search of prospects. Contact a local direct-mail company in your region. They can get you households headed by women with incomes in excess of $100,000, or environmentalists who live in a particular Zip Code or subscribers to Donors Anonymous Magazine (I made that one up). You rent the list. You'll be lucky if you break even on the appeal. But the donors you get are yours to be solicited again and again.

When someone responds to such a cold appeal, they're probably giving a fraction of what they could. Contact them, thank them, ask them what interests them about your work. Make a new best friend. But don't ask them for more money already. Wait until your next appeal.

ASK FOR MORE THAN YOU THINK THEY'RE LIKELY TO GIVE
One of the most generous philanthropists in the region told me to always ask people for more than you think they might give. He told me that affluent people are flattered when you think they are even more successful than they are. If you ask for too little, you'll get less than you might have. Don't be a pig, though.

GUESS WHO IMPORTANT PEOPLE (MEANING PROSPECTIVE MAJOR DONORS) WANT TO TALK TO?
They want to talk to the top person. An executive director who isn't willing to spend 30 percent or more of his or her time on fundraising is an executive director of an unsustainable organization or, at best, one that won't innovate and grow.

Chapter 12

Don't Call Me "President and CEO" and Other Lessons We Shouldn't Learn the Hard Way

IS THIS AN EGO THING? First of all, what is the difference between a "president" and a "CEO?" I would bet most nonprofit presidents and CEOs have no idea. "President and CEO" is a for-profit concoction. Why are the top dogs at nonprofits, large and small, using that title? Don't you think it makes you look self-promoting? Self-aggrandizing? How about self-absorbed? Wrong field? Ignorant?

Do you call your top fiscal manager a "CFO?" Is your IT guy a "CIO?" Is your chief volunteer officer, i.e., the top board member, the "chair of the board" and not the "president?" Is the staffer who manages the day-to-day operations a "COO?"

When folks in the community see that title are they impressed? Or do they think you're arrogant, even pompous? Hell, when I attend a meeting and am asked, along with everyone else, to introduce myself, I don't even identify myself as the executive director. Instead, I introduce myself as follows: "Hi, I'm Alan Jennings. I work for the Community Action Committee of the Lehigh

Valley." Anything more than that strikes me as a bit self-absorbed. I can see the top guy at the uppity local economic development corporation having that title, or the honcho at the hospital. But a little nonprofit theater? A Boys and Girls Club?

While I'm at it, do you push your board of directors to make your salary competitive with your peers in the nonprofit sector? Even worse, the private sector? Do you think prospective donors want to give to an organization whose top staffer looks like a corporate CEO, has a big house like their for-profit counterparts, or a flashy car? If you believe so, you must be lying to yourself. While some donors might think that way (I once had a donor give $10,000 and designate it to raising my salary; I refused and he never gave again), the vast number of regular folks, as well as elites, want to give to an organization that not only gets results, but is cheap as hell, a responsible steward of their community's money.

Among my proudest moments is when a reporter writes about the salaries of my peers and they are compared to mine. CACLV is one of the largest and most consequential nonprofits in my region, employing around 100 people, raising and managing a $25 million budget. We built it from nothing. And I've been the executive director for more than 28 years. I am paid just north of $100,000, well under my peers. Actually, that sounds like a lot. I get no agency-provided car and no country club membership (believe it or not, some do).

I'm not saying we should take a vow of poverty. I am saying that modesty and humility, when it comes to compensation, are appropriate. And virtue.It isn't virtuous for someone in service to others to be anything but clean.

Then there is the problem of income disparity. Even conservatives are starting to acknowledge that it isn't a good thing. So, why do nonprofit execs not understand that the multiple between the organization's top salary shouldn't be more than a factor of, say, six or seven?

Too many Americans are already cynical about their world. Government has been weakened and discredited by those on the Right who hate paying taxes (although plenty of folks in government haven't helped the cause). Our detractors cut our funding so we can't function effectively, then say, "See, government doesn't work!" They have fulfilled their own prophesy. And we let them.

Then we contribute our own evidence. Think about how many institutions that should be trusted by Americans have been discredited. Several years ago, the United Way of America was trashed because they lavished their top executive with all kinds of excessive perks.

The homophobia of the Boy Scouts didn't help the nonprofit sector's cause.

Too many hospitals make a ton of money, give far too little in charitable care to those in need, pay their top execs mountains of money. And, they enjoy nonprofit status.

Perhaps the most disgusting illustration is the Roman Catholic Church's pedophile scandal. They moved priests quietly to new parishes where they preyed on still more young people. The church felt that the preservation of the institution was more important than the health and safety of its children. Can it get any worse?

If you have a hard time making the distinction between right and wrong, that's God's way of telling you you're in the wrong field. One consideration is whether your actions can pass what I call the "reporter test." If there is any possibility that your behavior will fail muster in a news article, you might think twice about that behavior.

If you can't be the very definition of right versus wrong, stay in the for-profit sector. That's where reputations should go to be spoiled, not in our world. Sorry for the lecture, but, frankly, I'm sick of our work being taken down by the behavior of people who should know better.

Chapter 13

Where Did You Get the Idea That Lobbying is Illegal?

ONCE AND, HOPEFULLY, FOR ALL: A NONPROFIT ORGANIZATION UNDER SECTION 501(C)(3) OF THE INTERNAL REVENUE CODE CAN SPEND UP TO 20 PERCENT OF ITS BUDGET ON LOBBYING. That's right. Now, generally, you can't spend government funding on lobbying. But you can spend private funding (unless, of course, the donor specifies otherwise, which very, very few do). We have a $27 million budget, which means we can spend more than $5 million on lobbying. Honestly, we don't spend $4,000 on lobbying.

If you are paying even the slightest attention to what's going on in our world, I don't need to spend even a minute arguing why lobbying is important. You can run the best homeless shelter in America, but if Congress votes to cut the U.S. Department of Housing and Urban Development's public housing programs, nobody will be leaving your shelter anytime soon and within weeks your shelter will be practically useless.

MOST OF WHAT WE CALL LOBBYING IS ACTUALLY EDUCATION
"Lobbying" is the effort to influence others' decisions, most commonly applied to legislation. Technically, informing a legislator about an unmet need is not lobbying, nor is informing a legislator what damage will be done if a particular bill becomes law. You aren't "lobbying" until you take the next step and say, "Congressman, we need you to oppose House Bill 2143," or "Senator, please sign on as a co-sponsor of Senate Bill 1005."

HOLD A LEGISLATIVE FORUM
Organize a forum at which people who are affected by the bad legislative proposal that's out there give "testimony" to their experience. Invite all legislators (don't just pick Democrats, for example). Set up the room with one or more tables across the front, microphones at each seat or, at least, one for every two seats. Have someone from your organization lead the event, keeping it on track, properly organized and on message. Those who will be affected should tell their story and legislators given the opportunity to question those individuals and offer comments. Pick a room that you know is too small and pack it. Of course, invite the press. If some legislators are completely uncooperative, give each legislator a name tent and leave the tents of those legislators not in attendance in front of the empty seats. And don't forget to invite the press (I know, I already said that – this one was for emphasis).

This approach will get you press coverage. The indifferent legislators who failed to appear will look bad and even the cooperative legislators will make note of the consequences of not attending the next one. And make sure that there are at least some legislators who appreciate your tactic and will stick with you in the event that the offended offenders try to collude to get all the legislators to ignore the event.

In any event, use these kinds of tactics sparingly and carefully. Think about what could go wrong and how to mitigate that possibility. Moreover, the press could tire of this trick and stop cooperating.

Simplify your message to avoid confusing people and finding them taking the wrong side. Make your point very clear, maybe even to the point of repeating for emphasis. You can even say, "Folks, if there is a single, key point to be made, it is this…"

THIS STUFF ISN'T COMPLICATED
First, understand that the people we elect to represent us are not rocket scientists. They are, largely, us. I would argue that there are very few people in the not-too-swift Pennsylvania legislature who could get a real job that paid comparable wages to their cushy elected positions. Very few are much more

than glorified caseworkers. Many of them tend to get inebriated with their sense of self-importance but they are basically blind followers of their caucus leaders. So, they aren't going to take a lot of chances that might cost them those life-long benefits they'll get after serving just a few terms. I want to be clear: Many legislators, on both sides, are good, decent, reasonable, likable and, basically, pure. Just too many are not.

Here are some basic points that you should try not to forget (actually, carry this manual around at all times until it looks like a thoroughly worn out manifesto, then show it off to all your friends and colleagues):

- **Don't burn bridges**
  You might not get their support on everything you want; in fact, you might only get their support on occasion. But, you need that support, so don't do anything stupid like threaten to make sure they don't get elected again. Guess what? Chances are slim they won't win re-election, so empty threats will only ensure you never get their support.

- **Back yourself up with the facts**
  Emotional appeals might get you some sympathy, but it is important that you provide meaningful data to back up your position. Localize the data as much as possible. If you can give them data relevant to their specific constituents, that is ideal.

- **Don't offer support for their candidacy in their offices**
  That sounds like a bribe. Regardless, they are not allowed to campaign on government time or with government resources.

- **Get real people to tell their stories**
  Many "electeds" have the opinion that we lobby to protect our jobs or advance our careers. When you meet with an elected, take people who your organization serves with you so they can see and hear people's stories first hand. Obviously, it's best if you take people who are their constituents and, for that matter, registered to vote.

- **Get to know the elected's staff**
  They often understand the issues better than their boss does. Keep in mind, too, that, in the case of the state legislature or Member of Congress, they serve on committees that have their own staff. Those folks almost necessarily know the issues more than the legislator does, since they specialize in those that fall into the committee's jurisdiction, whereas legislators deal with just about every issue.

- **Make sure the elected knows how you can help them**
  Constituent service is an important part of what electeds do. Make sure they know what services you provide so they can refer their constituents to you.

  Then be sure to do your best with those constituents.

The frustrating part here is when electeds get credit for providing service even if they vote against funding your service. There isn't much you can do about that unless you have some guts. You can always write a letter to the editor of your local newspaper exposing their hypocrisy. But then you've burned that bridge. Use that sort of trick only after you've exhausted any hope of the elected being an ally.

SOME CONTACTS ARE BETTER THAN OTHERS
The Jennings Hierarchy of Effective Lobbying, least to most effective, with least at the top and most at the bottom:

- Petitions
- Blatantly organized campaigns with pre-printed postcards, form letters or identical emails
- Designated days where supporters of a cause call in on the same day for impact
- Personalized contact, such as your own letter, especially when it's handwritten
- Personalized phone call
- Meeting in the office of the elected
- Several prominent or grassroots supporters meeting with the elected (including bigger donors would help, too!)

ACTIONS YOU CAN TAKE THAT REQUIRE CAREFUL TREATMENT

Got guts? Apply them wisely.

Here's a risky tactic: publish the voting records of legislators in your area. Pick a bunch (read: a dozen or so) of legislative votes that were important to your constituency since the last election. Don't leave out key "procedural" votes, like a motion to kill a filibuster. Inform voters about how sympathetic "electeds" in your region are to the cause about which you care. Obviously, you're educating voters, who rarely even know that key votes took place, or what a "procedural" vote is. Knowledgable, smart voters, of course, are a great antidote for bad public policy.

The risk: you could appear partisan. Partisan political activity by nonprofits is strictly prohibited.

TO WHICH THE CONGRESSMAN RESPONDED, "ALAN, WHO THE HELL DO YOU THINK YOU ARE?"

My congressional district votes blue for president but is purple in every other way. We had a Democrat in the position for six years during the 1990s, the only one since 1978; a moderate, Paul McHale may be the most liberal Member of Congress we will ever get. I was deeply disappointed in his vote for welfare reform in 1996. When the inevitable phone call came from a reporter asking me what I thought about the congressman's vote, I was critical. Not stridently so, but critical. He was furious.

"Paul, if (former Republican Congressman) Don Ritter had voted that way I'd have held a press conference and gone for the throat."

"Alan, who the hell do you think you are?"

"I'm an advocate. I think you could argue that if I didn't criticize you for a vote that I think was harmful to poor people the Republicans would have a legitimate claim that my behavior was partisan and put my organization at risk," I said.

Friends, be careful.

Chapter 14

The Community Reinvestment Act

YOU HAVE TO LOVE A LAW THAT TAKES THE STUFFIEST, MOST CONSERVATIVE INDUSTRY IN OUR ECONOMY, ABSOLUTELY VITAL TO A HEALTHY MARKET, AND MAKES IT BEHOLDEN TO COMMIES LIKE ME. I don't think there could be a law in this country that is more underutilized but has more potential to transform our communities than this federal law.

In the early-1970's, activists in Chicago were catching anecdotal evidence that regulated financial services companies were not making loans in certain neighborhoods of the city. Chicago, you should know, is the center of the American universe when it comes to community organizing. Saul Alinsky, founder of the Industrial Areas Foundation and author of one of the great guides for community organizers, called Reveille for Radicals (get it, read it), operated out of Chicago, as did Gail Cincotta, founder of National People's Action.

Cincotta, something of a demi-god to neighborhood organizers, and her allies did the dirty work of tediously going through the public records for filing deeds and mortgages in Cook County, where Chicago is. They documented clear evidence of whole tracts of the city where banks weren't making loans. They alleged that bankers used red markers to identify those tracts. Thus, "redlining" was conceived.

Some bankers denied the accusation. Others argued that the Federal Housing Administration set up the circumstances that led to the practice. The devil made them do it!

It shouldn't be difficult to see why such practices would be devastating to urban neighborhoods. The notion that homeownership is critical to the health and vitality of a neighborhood is so widely understood that one shouldn't need to footnote the source. Conventional wisdom suggests that someone who owns is more likely to maintain it (nobody ever washes a rental car, you know), more likely to care about what else is going on around the neighborhood, more likely to participate, more likely to vote, more likely to call the police or join the PTA.

Senator William Proxmire, (D-WI), Chairman of the Senate Banking Committee, was convinced and, in 1977, the committee passed two laws in response to the claims made by Chicago's neighborhood activists.

The Home Mortgage Disclosure Act (HMDA) would require mortgage lenders to collect and report data to the regulators on who got loans and who didn't by income quintiles, census tract, race/ethnicity and gender.

Check it out: you can go to the website of the Federal Financial Institutions Examination Council (**www.ffiec.gov**) and find all kinds of data on who is and who isn't doing the right thing. You can dissect the data in all kinds of ways. You can look at it by income, census tract, race or gender; you can look at it by financial institution. You can look at the market collectively or by a segment. And, I guarantee you, you will find something that is disturbing. As my friends at the National Community Reinvestment Coalition, the trade association for CRA activists nationwide, like to say, "Data drives the movement." Facts are facts. These facts tell stories.

You can also get the data directly from a regulated bank. Of course, they are only required to provide you their own data. But, if you ask, it will get their attention. Then you're off on a campaign.

They know what they're doing that isn't good enough. When you start poking around, they'll be curious to know why. When you find something compelling, keep in mind the concept of "reputational risk." No industry is more sensitive to consumer or public relationships. Communities like the Lehigh Valley are saturated with bank services. While moving your money around is a pain, it can be done, and I'm convinced that plenty of people will move their money to a bank that demonstrates its commitment to that community better than other banks do.

In 1990, the Atlanta Journal-Constitution published a Pulitzer-winning story called, "The Color of Money." The reporter simply reported what the data showed and what millions of Americans already knew: White folks are the lucky folks in this great country. Indeed, people of color were about four times more likely to have their mortgage application rejected than their more fortunate counterparts.

It shook the industry. Banks scrambled to explain; they argued that the research didn't reflect differences in credit scores or down money.

So the Federal Reserve Bank of Boston did the tedious work of reviewing thousands of actual loan files, controlling for credits scores and other factors. There was still disparity. Not as bad, but bad enough.

In the Lehigh Valley, that set the stage for yours truly.

We looked at the data for our market. It looked as bad as or worse than Atlanta.

So I did what an activist who understands the power of the press would do: I gave the story to The Morning Call, our main daily newspaper. They did an outstanding job on the story, giving it the space it needed (an A-1 story, continued inside for two full pages). Some of the bankers trying to defend themselves looked silly. Our agency came out as the protagonist. We got their attention; they were now ready to talk, although they resented it.

Enter the Community Reinvestment Act. If HMDA provides the data to demonstrate that a community has a problem, CRA is the law that requires banks to solve the problem

The Community Reinvestment Act is anything but a household name. Even many non-profits and activists really don't know what it is. Given the power of this law, there is no excuse for communities to waste the opportunity to inject much more credit into struggling communities. But I've seen plenty of balls like this dropped by groups who ought to be paying better attention.

To Proxmire and his colleagues on the Senate Banking Committee, banks have special privileges, like government-sponsored deposit insurance, that obligate them to do good in the communities they serve. CRA requires banks to identify the unmet credit needs in their "assessment area," places where their presence requires them to meet those credit needs. And the law expects they will make an affirmative commitment to those low- to moderate-income communities and their residents.

For the first dozen years following the passage of the law, it had pretty minimal impact. The bank regulators never took it very seriously; they were more familiar with and concerned about safety and soundness regulations. Because the regulators were not particularly interested in something as commie-sounding as meeting the unmet credit needs of low-income communities, banks paid little attention. Enforcement of the law fell to communities that were being ignored. They were being ignored largely because the regulators were ignoring them. And activist groups lack sophistication and the resources to take on something as powerful as a corporation, especially one with a vault loaded with money. In larger communities where there was minimal overlap between rich people in power and alienated poor folks, activist groups were willing to challenge their banks, at least occasionally.

But in a community like the Lehigh Valley in Pennsylvania, where the bank president might be the chair of the board of the United Way or even sit at the other end of the pew from the non-profit exec, few CRA battles ever occurred.

Then a funny thing happened (funny in the sense of another disaster occurring because we learned nothing from the first several). You see, the Reagan Administration, in its zeal to undo all the good work that was done before it, deregulated the thrifts, or savings and loans, like the one George Bailey's family ran in the movie, "It's a Wonderful Life." Shockingly (not really), the industry got out of control and got into risky deals that hadn't been allowed since the last time some stupid president tried to cater to the industry. Before you know it, banks, which take regulation more seriously, were being forced to compete with the S&L's and started doing the same stupid deals.

Shazam! By 1988, the lessons were being learned all over again! And, once again, the government that so many people think gets in the way of commerce was coming to the rescue of an industry that was out of control. Yogi needs a new saying: déjà vu all over again and again and again and…

So, Congress cooks up a taxpayer-funded bail-out of these bozos. I'm guessing that the folks needing the bail-out probably wouldn't want to pay the bills of ordinary Americans who lose their job due to no fault of their own, but, sure! this is a great use of taxpayers' money!

Enter Henry Gonzalez, congressman from Texas who chaired the House Banking Committee, and Joe Kennedy, way cool dude from Massachusetts (that's right, one of those Kennedys). They wanted banker blood in exchange for the taxpayers' blood. So they demanded that CRA be strengthened. They were successful in making two very significant changes. First, the ratings that regulators give banks for how well they are meeting their obligations under CRA would now be public information. OOH! Reputational risk writ large, really large! Second, the regulators would now be able to push back on mergers due to lousy CRA performance, rather than the guy who runs a nonprofit funded by the United Way that is headed by the banker.

WHERE WERE WE? OH, YES, DISPARATE MORTGAGE LENDING
No surprises here in the Lehigh Valley where mortgage lending was as disparate as elsewhere. But we had another problem: Very few people of color were even applying for a mortgage. They knew what the outcome would be; why bother?

So, having gotten the banks' attention (they resented it but they went along with it) we all got together to discuss what we could do to correct the problem. Some banks were more committed than others. The committed banks became natural peer pressure.

We had already created a second mortgage product that covered down payments and closing costs but the program was minimally utilized for the reason stated above. It was clear we had more work to do.

We created what we called the Home Ownership Counseling Program (yes, I know, we lack creativity in naming our programs). The banks provided us funding to hire staff to conduct outreach in low-income and/or minority neighborhoods. We did old-fashioned, street-walking, flyer-distributing, poster-hanging outreach. We pointed out that households paying more than about $500 a month for a rental unit could probably own their own home for about the same amount.

We developed seminars conducted over three consecutive Saturdays on how to navigate the complicated process of buying a home. Volunteers with expertise in all the elements of the process, from the role of a real estate agent to how to finance the purchase to improving your credit score, conducted most of the training. People who attended all three of the sessions would get a certificate verifying that they had graduated.

We also got many of the banks to create special mortgage products that would include such features as lower interest rates, smaller down payments, tolerance for lower credit scores and forgiving some of the fees. However, in order to be eligible, the prospective homebuyer had to be lower-income (meaning total household income was below 80 percent of the area median income) and have a certificate confirming they had, indeed, graduated from our program. The banks' tolerance for lower down payments was based on the notion that attending our seminars was a form of sweat equity. It also meant the homebuyer had a pretty good sense of what they were getting themselves into.

But there was more. We needed, for our own credibility with the population we serve, some assurance that if we delivered the industry bankable homebuyers the industry would abandon whatever internal systems led to the disparate approvals. So, we insisted that participating banks have an internal second review to make sure that if the underwriter was rejecting a mortgage application for any of the wrong reasons someone else in the bank might catch it and correct it.

But there was still more. We stole an idea from our friends at the Philadelphia Urban League, called the Philadelphia Mortgage Plan. We recruited enough lenders that represented approximately 60 percent of the region's mortgage lending to participate in a peer review process. Any borrower whose circumstances fit into the reporting categories of the Home Mortgage Disclosure Act whose mortgage application the originating lender intended to reject would be brought before the peer group before issuing the rejection. The peer banks would challenge the originator on their decision. If the originating bank stuck with their decision to reject (after the internal second review), any of the participating banks in the plan would be allowed to take that application off the hands of the originating, rejecting bank. These peer-reviewed sessions would occur weekly under the watchful eye of one of the nonprofits in our housing coalition. Within a very short period of time, the rejections dropped dramatically.

The result? Between 1992, when we exposed the disparate mortgage lending, and 1996, the disparity was reduced from a factor of five to just 30 percent greater likelihood of rejection. That disparity could easily be explained by such legitimate circumstances as credit score or down payment. This was a stunning success. In fact, we shut down the Lehigh Valley Mortgage Plan after barely one year because so few rejections were occurring.

In just a few years, with the support of our new best friends in the banking industry, we had literally changed the complexion of home ownership in the Lehigh Valley.

Got your attention? Let's go back a bit and fill in some important stuff here.

PUBLIC EXPOSURE

Picture your favorite bank executive in one of those poses where they are buck naked but trying to hide the key spots. Not a pretty sight, and I don't mean to embarrass any of the folks working for the bank, but this really is a fair caricature of how exposed to public scrutiny these guys are.

First, they are publicly-traded companies, so their laundry is out for everyone to see: how much they get paid, how they made their money, and lots of other information. Second, the Home Mortgage Disclosure Act requires them to tell everyone who got mortgages and who didn't. Third, they have data that is publicly available on their small business lending. Fourth, their CRA rating is public information. Fifth, the regulators make a chunk of their report on how the bank meets its CRA obligation public. Sixth, they are required to keep a "public file" in which correspondence, including thank-you letters, must be kept for the public, as well as the regulators to see. Seventh, CRA exams are publicly announced and the public can comment at that point on the bank's performance. Eighth, when they change the nature of their business, such as buy another bank or are bought, or even when they want to open or close a branch, these actions are subject to public scrutiny and public comment. What they might prefer to hide is too big to cover with that little fig leaf. But they are good sports about it.

So, not only do they give us fodder for our canons, but they are even required to let us know when we should shoot. This extraordinary combination creates enormous opportunities to work with banks in a (mostly) collaborative environment.

BANKS GET RATINGS ON HOW WELL THEY COMPLY WITH THE LAW
As part of their compliance examination, banks are rated on a scale of 1 to 4: a "1" is "Outstanding," a "2" is "Satisfactory," a "3" is "Needs to Improve" and a "4" is "Substantial Noncompliance." The vast majority, well into the 90th percentile, receive Satisfactory or Outstanding ratings. This is a source of discontent among many CRA activists. However, just the fact that this ranking system exists puts pressure on banks to perform. Frankly, I am proud of the number of banks in our market that have outstanding CRA ratings, because it is a reflection of the value of the work we have done as well as the quality of the people who work in banks in our market. Our regional economic development corporation recently hired a consultant who, in the course of their work, identified the region's strengths. One of those was access to capital. We'll be happy to accept some of the credit for that, thank you very much.

CRA EXAMINATIONS ARE AN OPPORTUNITY TO WEIGH IN
When a bank is being examined under the Community Reinvestment Act, regular folks like us have an opportunity to comment. Really, the opportunity exists whether the bank is undergoing an examination or not. They are required to keep a "public file" at all times. This file is available for public scrutiny and you can write to the bank about almost anything related to their community reinvestment effort and you should find that correspondence in the file. That correspondence, then, is reviewed by the bank examiner.

Once again, the Federal Financial Institutions Examination Council is where you go for important information. For example, each quarter each regulator (the Federal Reserve, the Office of the Controller of the Currency, and the Federal Deposit Insurance Corporation) issues a list of banks whose CRA examinations will begin. You can access the FFIEC at **www.ffiec.gov**.

KNOW WHO THE KEY CONTACT IS
Every bank has a key contact in your market for CRA-related issues. That person is typically called the "CRA officer." They tend to be the token liberal at the bank and the person most likely to know what the hell is going on. They often come from our world and are sympathetic to our cause. You want to make friends with that person. And while you are at it, make sure you tell them you are a one-person job security program.

BANKS ARE TESTED ON LENDING, INVESTMENT AND SERVICE
Most banks are rated on how well they perform under three different tests: Lending, Investment and Service. The intent of the law is to ensure banks are not discriminating against poor people or their neighborhoods, so the lending test is the most important by far. In fact, a bank cannot get an outstanding rating unless they have an outstanding rating on their lending test.

HMDA data, consequently, is critical, since a mortgage is what I call the "gateway drug" to creating wealth. It is the most likely tool that the average family has for gaining an asset, or wealth. The equity in that house is the most likely collateral that anyone will use for improving the house, planning a bigger house, borrowing money to send your kids to college or even starting a business. How a bank performs on mortgage lending may be the most telling. Small business lending would certainly be the next most important indicator.

Examiners want to see that banks are making loans throughout their "assessment area." In other words, they must make loans in the poor folks' neighborhoods just as much as they do in the neighborhoods where the rich white folks get to live.

The investment test is a little more difficult to explain. Frankly, there is a pretty fine line between an "investment" and a loan. Moreover, the law requires and the examiners look for some degree of "creativity" in these investments. The reality is that very few banks really understand what is expected of them and they have difficulty complying.

By the way, the bank's philanthropy falls under the investment test. It is very important to understand and most people who have even the slightest idea what CRA is about don't: CRA is about lending and investments, not about charity. In fact, the bank's contributions play a fairly minor role as far as the law and those who conduct compliance examinations are concerned.

Finally, the "service test" looks at whether the services offered to customers are consistent across the assessment area. The location of the bank's branches are a key factor here. Also, the hours those branches are open matter. So, if a bank conveniently has its branches in suburban municipalities (in other words, higher income census tracts) but has none in urban (meaning lower-income) communities, the examiners should be noting that. If branches close before dark in minority census tracts (assuming they even have a branch in a minority census tract) but are open after dark in white census tracts, somebody ought to be noticing that.

THE "ASSESSMENT AREA"
The bank determines the boundaries of its assessment area based on where they are doing business. If a bank conveniently leaves lower-income and/or minority census tracts out of its assessment area, the regulators might have something to say about that.

We have a bank, headquartered in the market just south of us, that has been doing expeditionary raids in our market for several years. They have no branches and no other services in this market. But they have been cherry picking commercial loans out of the market. We hear estimates in the $100 million neighborhood. That strikes this CRA activist as a form of redlining. I hinted to their top executive here (not surprisingly, a commercial lender), that we were watching. I gave them a little time because, geez, we wouldn't want to be unfair to anyone, then contacted their CRA officer. We had breakfast. She was a nice enough lady but when I asked what they do to comply with the law, she told me that they donate to the Boys and Girls Club. Ahem. That's so nice. We parted on friendly terms.

To be fair, I waited a couple years. I saw no sign that the bank had gotten religion. So, I sent the bank's CEO the following letter (again, to be fair, redacted):

Dear Mr. [Bank Big Shot]:
The Community Action Committee of the Lehigh Valley has worked closely with banks in our market for many years to ensure that the partnership between the industry and the housing, community and economic development organizations serving this region effectively meets the credit needs of low- to moderate-income households and their neighborhoods. For some time we have monitored [FAIRNESS REDACTION]'s penetration into this market.

Our observation is that the bank has aggressively pursued commercial lending opportunities, booking well in excess of $100 million in such loans. However, my impression is that [FAIRNESS REDACTION] has avoided products and services that are important in meeting the bank's obligations under the Community Reinvestment Act. While the bank has built an office in South Whitehall Township, it has no retail presence in the market, including the LMI [low- to moderate-income] census tracts that are almost exclusively located in our urban communities or even in the central business districts of our cities.

I have seen no sign of the bank promoting mortgage products that are critical to enabling households with incomes in the lower quintiles to build assets and wealth. With the exception of the placement of an ad in CACLV's most recent Annual Report (which we deeply appreciated), I have seen little sign of outreach in LMI communities.

A few years ago I had the pleasure of meeting [THE CRA OFFICER] to learn more about the bank's plans as it grew its presence in this marketplace. My impression taken from that conversation was that the bank felt it was meeting its community reinvestment obligations by making donations to non-profits providing services in LMI neighborhoods. While we all appreciate charitable contributions, as you know, those contributions play a very small role in the regulators' review of a bank's performance, favoring, instead, the extension of credit through lending and investments.

I would appreciate the opportunity to meet with you to get a better understanding from the top of the company how [FAIRNESS REDACTION] meets its community reinvestment obligations in the Lehigh Valley where the bank appears to be much more interested in lucrative commercial lending than it is in responding to the credit needs of ordinary people and their neighborhoods. In preparation for such a meeting, I would appreciate it if you would send me the public disclosure report from your last CRA examination as well as any outreach materials you might have that promote the bank's products and services that are available in the Lehigh Valley market.

I have enclosed our aforementioned 2014-2015 Annual Report in case you had not seen it. I hope you can find a minute to take a look at it to learn more about our work.

I look forward to the opportunity to discuss the bank's plans for this market.

Sincerely,

I gave the CEO, continuing to be fair, more than two months to respond. Nothing. So, I sent the following letter:

Dear Mr. [Bank Big Shot Who Doesn't Seem to Realize He's Being Set Up]:
I wrote to you in early November asking for an opportunity to meet to discuss the bank's plans to meet its community reinvestment obligations in the Lehigh Valley, given its active pursuit of commercial business but little attention to retail and no apparent attention to the Community Reinvestment Act. As of this writing, I have not received a response. Perhaps you never received that letter; if not, I have enclosed a copy.

I look forward to the opportunity to meet. If you are willing, please contact Amanda Newell at anewell@caclv.org or by calling the phone number captioned on this letterhead. Also, I would appreciate a copy of the public disclosure report from your last CRA exam.

Thanks for your attention to this second request.

Sincerely,

I would give him a month. If I would get no response, fairness would no longer be so important.

After the month passed I contacted the examiners at the Fed in Philadelphia to make sure I was on solid ground.

Harrumph! I wasn't! I was reminded that the whole point of CRA is to get capital into your community. So, small business loans, even loans that have no obvious benefit to lower-income communities, are a good thing. The community that was being short-changed was the one where the bank was headquartered, since the deposit base was funding loans in another community. So, to challenge this bank we would have to give the story to the bank's hometown newspaper. It's on my list of things to do but, frankly, it isn't a priority. One would think that the Fed will raise this issue with the bank during its next CRA exam. But it still bugs me that the bank is doing small business lending here but not doing retail banking or mortgages in the 'hood.

THE WHOLE PROCESS IS PRETTY SUBJECTIVE
There are no specific standards by which to measure a bank's performance under the law. The examiners have considerable leeway in their reviews. What they are looking for are disparities. As the reader can understand, this makes banks a little crazy. However, it means there is plenty of room to work this issue.

MERGERS ARE THE BEST LEVERAGE YOU HAVE FOR GETTING THE BANKS' ATTENTION
While it appears that mergers and acquisitions are approved without contention, this is an opportunity to challenge a bank to do better and to build a relationship that could be productive for decades to come. During the merger process the news media are paying more attention to the bank. Also, there is a public comment period that allows for aggrieved interests to challenge the bank's merger on CRA grounds. Inevitably, the bank will want to talk – too much money is at stake.

This dance is a very careful one – not a breakdance but more like a waltz. Keep in mind that you want to establish a working relationship for years to come – pushing too hard might work in the short-term but a productive, longer-term relationship is all about, well, relationships. Another complication is that the window is open for a very short period of time. Too much patience will blow the leverage you have if you don't get something accomplished before the comment period ends.

We have this dance here in the Lehigh Valley almost every time a merger is announced. We have a coalition of just about all of the community, housing and economic development groups, including the cities of Allentown, Bethlehem and Easton and both Northampton and Lehigh counties. We invite the CEO or, if the bank is so big nobody has ever met him (sorry, but the only female CEO we have met is Beth Mooney from Key Bank, headquartered in Cleveland), we invite the top CRA official to the market for some discussions.

At the first meeting, we get to know each other a little by talking about what we do, exchanging business cards and information about our groups. We ask the bank to talk about their company, tell us what interested them in our market, how they're organized and what their plans are for meeting their CRA obligations. We talk about the unmet credit needs in our community.

Then, we offer to hold a press event to welcome them and celebrate their entry into our market. However, we want to tell the public what it is about the bank that makes them worthy. That's when we seek another meeting with the bank to discuss the issues we would like to see them address. If they commit to enough products and services, we will hold the media event.

We have done this so many times, it is practically pro forma. Our relationships are so good with the banks that the CEO of the acquired bank usually buys in, setting up communication with the top execs at the new bank and encouraging them to cooperate. After one of the meetings, the CEO and his top lieutenant were hanging around, just the three of us talking. I said, "I'm assuming you checked me out." He had. "Who did you talk to?" The Secretary of the Pennsylvania Department of Banking. The secretary had been the CEO of one of the banks in our market with which we danced. That can't hurt our cause.

The document that comes out of these discussions is always publicly disclosed. We call it a "commitment." In the old days we called them "agreements" and they were signed by all parties. We got away from that approach because it felt like nobody trusted each other. And, besides, there is no entity that can enforce the agreement. So, we call them commitments and work at the partnership to accomplish as much as we can.

In the appendix you will find an actual commitment we developed with one of our banks in this market. Take a look; what community wouldn't be thrilled to have that kind of commitment from one of the top banks in its market? Unfortunately, due to a provision that requires such "agreements" or "commitments" to be disclosed to the regulators and regular reports filed on progress against the deal, this bank did not want the commitment publicly released. Considering that the very disclosure of the commitment reinforces the culture of cooperation and progressive CRA implementation that has been established in our market, I was not happy about the bank's resistance to disclosure, but I capitulated. Given the outstanding CRA rating both the acquirer and the acquired had, I felt that we should give them that break.

CRA IS ABOUT PARTNERSHIPS, NOT EXTORTION
A lot of people would have a hard time mustering much sympathy for banks. But some community groups have played CRA almost as if it gave us a license to extort resources from the banks. I do not take that approach. CRA, in order to be effective, must result in partnerships between community groups who understand their communities' credit needs as well as the challenge of doing community development since many of us have been practitioners. Partnerships don't thrive when one group bullies the other, or one group has the bat and ball and might quit and go home. So the dance with banks is a very careful one. If done right it can be quite a beautiful thing. If done wrong, the decline of the community will quicken because a community will struggle without effective community reinvestment.

But don't be afraid. To be clear, our approach is to reinforce responsible community reinvestment rather than threaten punishment if the bank doesn't concede; our experience is that you don't have to go that far.

THERE IS AN EXTREMELY IMPORTANT ROLE HERE FOR A CATALYST, CHANGE AGENT, COALITION-BUILDER, COMMUNITY PROBLEM-SOLVER, ADVOCATE OR WHATEVER YOU WANT TO CALL IT
Get the troops together. Speak with one voice. If you don't have something close to unanimity, it will be too easy to divide and conquer. Try to cut everyone in. This is not about you getting all you can for your organization; it's about community. The more selflessly you pursue this campaign the more respect you'll gain and

the easier it will be to get their support for your own initiatives. For example, the banks in our market need help reaching people who have historically been rejected for loans, people who stopped trying out of frustration. So, they should fund outreach campaigns, homeownership counseling programs, entrepreneurial training, financial literacy. Those are great services to add to your arsenal. You'll have to find other funding to complement the banks' support, but their funding is a great start.

The benefits to you and your organization are significant. Whenever a compliance exam is conducted by the regulators, they'll contact you. The banks will know that. One local bank got its first-ever outstanding CRA rating and the CEO called me to thank me. He knew they wouldn't have gotten the rating if I hadn't been so supportive. Conversely, you can hurt a bank during a compliance exam. Also, whenever there is a merger, the media is likely to contact you, seeing you as an expert on the bank's role in the community and wanting to know how the merger will change that role. You'll get invited to their holiday parties, where the glitterati will be present and you can schmooze them and, if you know what you're doing, turn them into supporters, hopefully even donors.

AND WHAT DO THE BANKS THINK ABOUT ALL OF THIS?
Let's face it – not a lot of banks would go to the trouble to extend credit to lower-income people and their neighborhoods if the law didn't require it. I don't fault them for that. I'd like to think all bank CEO's are do-gooders dressed like bankers, driving cars like bankers, keeping golf schedules like bankers, living in big houses like bankers but with big hearts yearning to make their community a better place.

Many of these guys (you still won't find a lot of women at the top), though, have found religion and, at the very least, say the right things about reinvesting in their communities. They hate the mandates, hate the paperwork, hate the compliance exams. But they recognize that they can't make any money in a depressed community. And there aren't enough La La Lands anymore. So, to all the wannabe change agents reading this book, get your ass out there. This one is a relatively easy win.

Chapter 15

Advocacy

BY DEFINITION, AN ADVOCATE IS ONE WHO SPEAKS FOR OR ON BEHALF OF ANOTHER. There are plenty of reasons why we need advocates, although I wish there was not a single one. I wish each and every one of us, given the promise of democracy, had a voice, that we knew how to use it, we knew how to amplify that voice, how to bring together many voices in unison or even harmony to demand better for ourselves. Alas, our system does not lend itself very effectively to such a wish. Not everyone is comfortable challenging the system. Not everyone understands the rules. Not everyone has the resources to grease the skids and get politicians to pay attention. Not everyone speaks the language of power. Not everyone can find the words. Not everyone has the self-esteem to feel sufficiently self-confident to seize an opportunity. Not everyone is able-bodied. And not everyone has any confidence that their voice would make anything better. That's called hopelessness.

And so, justice, if we are to embrace the concept, would demand that we not leave someone behind simply because they lack the guts or the ability or even the desire to stand up for themselves. Let's talk about how that gets done.

ASSESSING THE NEED
It can be pretty embarrassing to speak on someone else's behalf and get your facts wrong. Getting them right, communicating them effectively to find allies, sympathizers, donors, elected officials and others who move and shake the system is a key element of effective advocacy. Knowing that those on behalf of whom you are speaking trust you and are counting on you are key elements of effective advocacy.

Using the news media to educate the public is also helpful, since politicians and most other community leaders also watch the news to better understand their constituency and to see what issues are getting attention. High-profile advocacy campaigns can be a good way to get your electeds' attention. In fact, getting anyone's attention is helpful, as you never know who's watching.

Essentially, you are generating "chatter" about the cause. Good work. Now do something with it.

ARMED WITH DATA, TAKE ACTION

Identify the prospective good guys; they should be respected. They should have energy and enthusiasm for the cause. They should have power. And resources (or access to resources).

Identify the causes of the need, including who the bad guys are.

Get the good guys together. Chat. Are these issues important enough to you? Are you willing to be part of the solution? Let's talk tactics.

DON'T RECRUIT WIMPS

I'm not saying you only want people with testosterone coursing through their bodies. I am saying that you need people with a backbone, people who are resolved, people who are willing to throw a high, inside fastball, if necessary. People in our field tend to be tolerant; they try to see, consider and put themselves in the position of others in the debate. Get over that. People in positions of power can afford to be genteel. We can't.

They say that patience is a virtue. I don't agree. Patience is the luxury of the powerful, the affluent, the comfortable. Don't be patient on behalf of those who can make no such claims.

Like board recruitment, find people and constituencies that have a stake in the outcome, as well as people who don't. Find people with expertise in the issue you are confronting, find people who are connected in some way to the obstacle to getting things moving forward. Find workers.

Someone or some entity will have to provide the staff support. Volunteers are more effective when they aren't burdened with the hassles of scheduling meetings, taking minutes or any other tedious tasks. I hate that uncomfortable moment when you ask who would be willing to take notes in the meetings and everyone's eyes look down or start darting, hoping nobody catches them. That split second can feel like minutes of agony: You can do it, no, I really don't want to and please don't try to make me feel guilty, but you're the only one here who cares enough about this stuff and understands its importance, perhaps, but I really don't want to volunteer for this, please don't ask.

THERE ARE NO TACTICAL BOILERPLATES

Every such effort is going to have its own, unique situation. It will be up to the group to collectively determine how to proceed at each step along the way. At each step, then, the group will have to determine how long to wait, when a proposal becomes pressure and when pressure turns into the high, inside fastball (I can't resist baseball metaphors) and when, if ever, the high, inside fastball becomes a beanball (sorry, couldn't resist). In my opinion, the other side should always have the impression that a beanball is one of your best pitches that you should try your best not to use.

"FAMILIES IN TRANSITION"

In the mid-1980s, as the American economy was coming out of its nastiest recession in 50 years, much had changed. Massive numbers of industrial jobs with union wages and benefits were lost forever. Health benefits, in particular, were getting shaved by employers in the interests of controlling labor costs and competing in a more global economy. Large numbers of unemployed workers exhausted their unemployment benefits. The incidence of families lacking health insurance was on the rise.

Meanwhile, "health networks" were beginning to form. In the Lehigh Valley, the earliest iteration of the trend that continues to this day was the creation of an entity called HealthEast, which has evolved today into Lehigh Valley Health Network, the region's biggest employer. I didn't know it at the time but the guy who conceived HealthEast was not only smart as hell and an expert at organizational development but he had very progressive politics, as did his wife, who became one of our best volunteers (they moved out of the area decades ago but still send us an annual contribution).

People hate change. They rarely understand it, never trust it and often come up with cockamamie ideas about motives. When change is proposed by someone who hasn't been living in the area for at least 30 years, it becomes all the more suspicious. That is a climate you can exploit.

I called the CEO. Normally, in a situation like this, you would have to identify someone who is an ally and knows the individual you are trying to influence. You contact that ally, you ask for help and, inevitably, you get some. It might be nothing more than a "feel free to use my name when you contact him" or might be an offer to facilitate an introduction directly, maybe over lunch. I was only 28, was already pretty widely reputed as a troublemaker and probably shouldn't have gotten the time of day. But I did – I got both the date and time for a meeting.

A parallel development at the time, given all the chatter about the evolving health care situation, was growing suspicion of the entity folks started to call "HealthBeast." I had publicly wondered whether this entity was pursuing some kind of nefarious overthrow of all things good in the region (OK, that may be a bit of an exaggeration but, hey, I was contributing to a climate that could be conducive to getting some good things accomplished). Those of us carrying pitchforks and torches even started to raise the question of whether the health system's tax exemption should be challenged.

You want to get a big nonprofit to pay attention? Challenge its tax exemption. The threat alone can be productive. If you have a sympathetic judge, you can really get some good action.

Let's look at a college. With the exception of the rise of for-profit schools like Phoenix or Strayer, almost all institutions of higher education are tax-exempt. But why? The college that's in my neighborhood is encroaching into the neighborhood, in the process following so many other schools that have done great damage. Nobody wants to live next to a bunch of rowdy college students. Hell, I would not have wanted to live next to me when I lived off-campus one year. Beer cups. Parties with literally 100 or more kids in the house. No respect for limited parking spaces. They don't cut the grass, rake the leaves or shovel their snow. They don't put their trash out properly. They don't take their trash cans in after the trash has been collected. It is amazing how effective they are at reducing property values, which fits perfectly into the college's plans for buying still more properties. Before you know it, you're surrounded, the value of your home is in the tank and nobody wants to buy it except for the tax-exempt institution that cheapened it.

This college fancies itself an elite school and is far more likely to grant admission to a kid from Seattle than a kid from down the street. Yes, they create jobs but so do a lot of entities that don't receive a tax exemption. So, why should a county or city grant tax exemption to an entity that provides little benefit to the local community but still requires local services for which it pays nothing. Now, keep in mind, this is not one of those "consensus bad guys." There are lots of alum who stick around after graduating, and employees and their families vote.

That tax-exempt status makes them an easy target. Sic 'em!

Back to our healthcare advocacy effort. I have no idea how much the public chatter and the developing challenge to the health system's tax status factored into the thinking of the CEO, but this guy turned out to be great to work with. He understood all of the calculus and I barely needed to remind him of the big picture.

We proposed that the system provide free health care to people who were uninsured. Knowing that providing care to everyone was a non-starter, the question for me was whether we could use this service to incentivize or reward certain behavior. So, we proposed that the free health care be provided to those families where the head of household was unemployed, the household consequently was uninsured and the unemployed head of household was participating in the job training and job placement services offered by the local workforce development organization called the Private Industry Council. After some planning that included PIC staff, HealthEast staff and CACLV, we launched a pretty impressive effort called Families in Transition. The health system, at its own expense, provided health care to 400 families at a time. The program lasted for several years and eventually was absorbed into the hospital's routine services.

After the health system agreed to provide services to the prison population, the tax-exempt challenge went away.

THEN THERE ARE THE REALTORS

Easy target, don't you think? Did you see "American Beauty" with Kevin Spacey and Annette Benning? The Realtor who called himself "The King of Real Estate" was perfect, wasn't he?

For years we had heard anecdotes of prospective white homebuyers being steered out of buying a home in the city of Allentown by Realtors. They would disrespect the school district, the crime, the people who didn't look like them, the high property taxes.

One time I got myself on the agenda of one of their board meetings. They had stopped contributing to our homeownership counseling program, which puts educated homebuyers into the market. Yes, here we were introducing hundreds of new customers into the market each year and the Association of Realtors, which once was contributing more than $10,000 per year, was giving us a big, fat, goose egg. Nada. Nil. Zippo. Zilch.

So, I got on their monthly agenda. At the meeting, one of their members referred to one of the people we served as a "colored guy." OK, the picture is getting clearer.

Allentown Mayor Ed Pawlowski and I talked about this problem off and on over several years. Finally getting enough, he offered us some federal Community Development Block Grant funding to organize a testing program. In federal fair housing circles, "testing" is an effective and well-established approach for busting those who think it is OK to discriminate against people in housing situations.

Volunteers are trained in how to pose as prospective homebuyers and document the behavior they experienced. Some of the volunteers represent "protected classes," such as people of color or people with disabilities.

In each test, someone from a protected class and someone who is not both approach a Realtor, telling them that they want to buy a house in "the city of Allentown," not the suburban municipality next door in the same zip code but in the city's boundaries. The testers present comparable income, length of employment and credit scores. They call a Realtor and it's off to the races.

We hired the Fair Housing Council of Suburban Philadelphia (now called the Housing Equality Center of Pennsylvania). They have extensive experience in doing testing and were dying to come about 40 miles north to pick some fights. I knew the director from our common membership in the National Community Reinvestment Coalition.

We set up the process and waited for the results. It was ugly.

We conducted 33 tests. Out of those, 74 percent were determined to be "conclusive" violations of the Fair Housing Act. Twenty-three percent were deemed to be "inconclusive." Only one test of the 33, just 3 percent of those tested, was considered to be "conclusively" in compliance with the law.

Unbelievable. The director of the Fair Housing Council told me these were the worst results in his 33-year career. He said it harkened back to the kind of results they's seen in Philly in the 1950's.

When a community group nails someone or some company on a fair housing complaint, that gives it standing in the case and it can sue and recover compensation in the matter. The Fair Housing Council wanted to conduct more tests and build a case for a suit.

I got the mayor to agree that, instead of suing, we should engage the Lehigh Valley Association of Realtors. That 74 percent is stunning and suggests that the whole industry was guilty, not just a few "bad apples."

Keep in mind that anyone who owned property in the city of Allentown was a victim of wealth-stripping. Let's just go through the Econ 101 of this situation. If those most likely to get a mortgage (i.e., white homebuyers) are being steered out of the market, reducing demand for properties in that market, then pressure on prices will decline. Those prices represent value and, therefore, equity. Consequently, as an Allentown homeowner, my equity is being stripped.

If you take those same homebuyers and move them over to this other market, that increased demand will result in increased pressure on prices upward, resulting in increased equity and, therefore, wealth. This is a classic example of why there is such historic wealth disparity in this country.

So this is serious stuff. But I felt that we should confront the Realtors with the smoking gun and press them to work with us to correct the systemic problem. The Fair Housing Council rep expressed doubt that the Realtors would cooperate, saying they never have. I felt otherwise.

I called the CEO of the association and told him I wanted to meet and that he should bring their attorney along. He wanted to keep it just between him and me. I agreed. We met. He agreed to discuss how they can right the wrong. I was proud to report back to my colleague in Philly that this community is different than many others; the association, indeed, agreed to concede that they have a problem they want to correct.

Discussions took place over a couple months. While we didn't get everything we sought, the association was pretty cooperative, including agreeing to a joint press conference where they would admit to having problems and announce concessions. There is something about the Lehigh Valley that makes it unique. We think we probably deserve a little bit of credit for that culture.

> **HERE IS A PARTIAL LIST OF THE ACTIONS THE GREATER LEHIGH VALLEY REALTORS ASSOCIATION AGREED TO TAKE:**
> - Create a diversity task force that would oversee all activities designed to correct the issues we raised; include a community representative from outside the LVAR;
> - Work with the mayors of the three cities to promote housing sales in Allentown, Bethlehem and Easton;
> - Hand out information to prospective buyers explaining their rights under the Fair Housing Act;
> - Ask the licensed brokers to sign a pledge recommitting themselves to abide by the law on fair housing matters;
> - Make a special effort to recruit and train people of color into their ranks and discount the cost of membership.

We will surely do another testing campaign to keep the Realtors on their toes. My bet is that there will still be major problems. This time we'll sue, and they will not be able to make even the slightest claim that we weren't fair. We won't criticize the entire industry but will challenge those individuals who demonstrate that they didn't learn a thing from the first testing project.

More recently, I learned that the National Association of Realtors was using this entire incident to train new realtors in Fair Housing practices.

Chapter 16

Raising Hell and Raising Money, Too

THERE IS A SCHOOL OF THOUGHT IN THE NONPROFIT WORLD THAT ASSERTS THAT BEING OUTSPOKEN, FIGHTING THE GOOD FIGHT, DOING COMMUNITY PROBLEM-SOLVING AND POLICY ADVOCACY WORK WILL SCARE AWAY DONORS WHOSE VIEWS MIGHT BE INCONSISTENT WITH YOURS OR WHO DON'T APPRECIATE NONPROFIT ADVOCACY. Baloney. I would argue that raising hell and raising money go hand in hand.

I really believe that most people care about their neighbors, including their neighbors in need. Few, though, have or take the time to do the due diligence to find a good vehicle for making a difference. As you will read on other pages, the most important skill in raising hell is the effective use of the news media. Getting attention is a critical part of raising money, too; if people don't know you exist, they won't think about you when it comes to volunteering or making a donation.

Even when they don't entirely agree with your outspokenness, most Americans respect resolve, especially among their leaders. Polls consistently showed that American public opinion was not aligned with either Ronald Reagan's or George W. Bush's agenda (how could they be?!) but they appreciated their presidents' resolve. Conversely, when John Kerry made the famous statement, "I actually voted for it [giving W. the authority to launch the most disastrous foreign policy mistake in American history] before I voted against it," his presidential campaign was doomed. Americans want to know what their leaders stand for. They hate wishy-washy, mealy-mouthed weenies pretending to be leaders.

CACLV is easily the most outspoken, hell-raisingest advocacy, community development and human services organization in the region and, yet, we have thousands of donors, including many of the top CEOs in the area, raising more than $4 million each year in operating support for our work. Many don't agree with some of our more controversial tricks but they appreciate the quality of our work, the seriousness of our commitment to responsible stewardship and our resolve. Admittedly, some give for fear of the consequences of the alternative. That's a lousy reason but, if it works, I'll take it.

So, here are some things to keep in mind when trying to raise money while you're raising some good, old-fashioned hell.

BE CLEAN AND GOOD
I've said it before, but you have to be good at what you do and spotless with your integrity. If you challenge the system – any part of it – you have to be sure that you can't be dismissed as lacking integrity. They will want to find a way to discredit and undermine you. Don't give them anything.

ORGANIZE A CAMPAIGN DIRECTED AT A CONSENSUS BAD GUY
Whatever you do, understand the consequences of picking on someone who is well-liked or whom folks are afraid to alienate. You can do it, but it's not wise as your first effort. You can take on a hospital for not doing enough charitable care while clearing millions in surpluses each year, but take a look at who's on the board of directors or look at their donor list. Then think twice.

Slum landlords are good targets. Not a lot of people like Realtors, but there are a lot of them and some of them must have friends and allies. Predatory lenders were chased away by their own excesses. Count on them to find some new dirty tricks. Payday lending is still legal in most states (not Pennsylvania, thanks, in part, to our work). Who likes those bastards? How about polluters? Walmart?

When you get good at this and you have a couple of high-profile wins, you can go after more risky targets, but start with the consensus bad guy. Keep in mind that the term "wins" is rather vague. Ending payday lending and getting the creeps to compensate those who have been ripped off would be the whole enchilada.

But even if all you get is a stack of news clippings that have been seen by a lot of people, you've gotten a win, because you will have gotten folks' attention. That attention might lead another possible target to fold and cooperate without much of a fight. But it will also impress the folks who are looking for a cause to which they can contribute.

WORK IN COALITION
I guarantee, if you follow this approach, you will regret it. I can also say, with confidence, that if you don't you will regret that even more.

Let me start with this: there aren't a lot of outstanding nonprofits or activist organizations fighting the good fight. When an organization does excel, the mediocrity of the pack comes into even clearer focus. That will result in professional jealousy. Some of those jealous folks might keep their opinions to themselves. Others will try to undermine you, discredit you, comment anonymously on the blogs or on news media websites.

If you invite them to the table, they might actually accept. They might learn something from you. They might like you and, jealous or not, feel too badly about dissing you. They might realize how beneficial the coalition approach is. The bad guys won't, then, be able to divide and conquer.

In fact, to make sure that other groups, friendly or not, do not take cheap shots, I think it is important to share the spoils of your advocacy or community problem-solving. Admittedly, this probably feels like you're buying friends. Maybe. I still think you need to do it.

My guess is that just about every reader of this book who is involved in the issue of homelessness lives in a community where the homeless shelters are located in the oldest, densest, most challenged neighborhood in your region. There are plenty of reasons for that, including that that is where the weakest resistance is, that is where the right kind of building that can be retrofitted into a homeless shelter will be located, it's where the cheapest buildings can be found and it's usually near other services to which homeless people can be referred.

Of course, you know that having a shelter nearby is not going to increase property values; the community that hosts the homeless shelter will lose tax base because the property will become tax-exempt. When an incident occurs at the shelter it is the host municipality's fire department, police department or health department that will respond to the incident. And it is the host municipality's funding, whether it is federal block grants or general fund revenue that will get squeezed to fund the shelter. Consequently, the entire burden of sheltering the homeless in a community ends up borne by the urban municipality, the municipality that already, typically, is where most poor folks call home. Meanwhile, out where the sun shines on the cul-de-sacs and the fine-trimmed lawns and the schools with the most funding are located, where many of the municipalities don't even have or need police departments, folks can live not only blissfully ignorant, but free of the costs of those pesky homeless people and their children.

Doesn't seem fair, does it? This sounds like another opportunity to poke your finger at the question of what is fairness in our society. We thought it worth raising that question and got the shelters together to do just that.

The housing coalition we created back in 1984 had been collecting extensive data on who our shelters were serving. We knew how many people were sheltered, how old they were, what they look like, where they came from, how old the moms were when they had their first child, whether they had high school degrees or a job and what kinds of services they were accessing. This kind of needs assessment is valuable when applying for grants, asking people for donations and educating voters. We weren't as surprised as the blissfully ignorant suburban folks were about where these unfortunate souls came from but having the data was powerful.

In the first year or two of collecting this data we realized we weren't asking the right questions. Almost all of the homeless people cited an urban community as their last address before becoming homeless. It dawned on us that the cities were where nearly all of the oldest, densest, most substandard and, of course, affordable housing was located. So, we added a question asking our shelter residents where they had ever lived and *(shazam!)* they had come from all around. Here was the pattern: they lived in a suburban community, became a

victim of many of life's challenges – they lost a job, or a spouse or their good health, forcing them to move into more affordable housing, meaning a city. Their struggles would be punctuated by more setbacks, like their car dying or their spouse beating them up. Before they knew it they were shaking their heads, tears running down their cheeks, trying to figure out how to tell their children what it meant to live in a homeless shelter.
Suddenly, we had powerful data that we could take to the township supervisors and commissioners who held the purse strings out there where the sun shines.

We began making the pitch and had more luck than one might imagine. Yes, there were plenty of municipalities in which the majority of "electeds" were quite content with their dug-in positions in opposition to doing the right thing but there were plenty of others whose sense of common decency was just as offended as ours was. We were raising $40,000 per year, enabling us to distribute several thousand dollars each year to each of the region's homeless shelters. In fact, while the city of Allentown remained the most common former home of people who would someday become homeless, the collection of suburban communities around us was second.

Unfortunately, few of the shelters lifted a finger to help us make the case. We found ourselves almost alone in making the pitch. Still, on principle we kept making the appeal each year, believing the suburbs needed to hear the argument and believing that we were making a moral one.

Indeed, coalitions are a challenge, especially for long-term problem-solving campaigns like our housing coalition's.

One of the most frustrating things about coalitions is that there is an inverse relationship between the amount of effort a member puts in and the return the organization (or individual) receives on that investment: Those who put the most effort in get the lowest ROI, while the groups that invest the least get the highest return. It's still worth it to engage in coalition work, but try to find ways to get groups to understand that fact of life and commit similar energy.

Chapter 17

There Are Plenty of Ways To Do It

HERE IS A FRACTION OF "PLENTY"

DO AN EXTENSIVE SURVEY OF THOSE WHOSE LIVES NEED EMERGENCY ASSISTANCE TO SURVIVE
Recruit volunteers from the community – a social mission committee of an active church might be a good source – or get one to three student interns. Get their sociology professor or the marketing director of a local company to develop a survey instrument (it's important to do this using respected industry tools). When the survey results are in, gather a small committee of various experts to interpret the results. Hold a press conference to present them. Share them with the food pantries, soup kitchens and homeless shelters so that they can become lucid in the results and, perhaps, find their way into the news stories.

CREATE A TASK FORCE TO MAKE IMPROVEMENTS TO THE BEHAVIORAL HEALTH SYSTEM
As a requirement of the Affordable Care Act, the hospital(s) in your community do a community health needs assessment every few years. I guarantee they conclude that your behavioral health system sucks. It sucks everywhere. Get the troops together and go see the folks who did the assessment and ask them whether you should be holding your breath in anticipation of the announcement of what great plans they have to fix it. When they give you that blank look, you'll have a fight to pick.

START A SERIOUS CAMPAIGN TO RAISE THE MINIMUM WAGE
You know you should be doing this anyway. For crying out loud: The best way to fight poverty is to get workers better wages. What are you waiting for?

CREATE A TASK FORCE TO GUARANTEE ALL 3- AND 4-YEAR-OLDS EARLY CHILDHOOD EDUCATION
Everyone knows that ECE should be an entitlement. Who is opposed to giving cute little kids a fair shake in preparing for a lifetime of learning?

BUG THE BANKS
Very few municipalities realize how huge the federal Community Reinvestment Act is in motivating banks to do more outreach in their local communities. So, it's a safe bet that your community is dropping the ball. You can create loan pools for affordable housing or small businesses, financial literacy, first-time homebuyer programs and so much more. Contact the National Community Reinvestment Coalition. They can help. Or I will!

START A CAMPAIGN TO PROMOTE CIVIC ENGAGEMENT
Solicit sponsors for an ad campaign designed to motivate your community to abandon its apathy and start getting involved. You can push volunteering, voting, or simply educate people about needs in their community.

START A FUND FOR YOUTH ACTIVITIES BY GETTING SENIORS TO DONATE THE SAVINGS FROM THEIR SENIOR DISCOUNTS
Seniors are, arguably, the most financially comfortable age cohort in America. And, yet, they are the beneficiaries of countless consumer discounts, on admission to movies, shows and all kinds of entertainment as well as many other products and services. Organize seniors to create the initiative, including promoting the donations and choosing how to distribute the proceeds.

Every one of these ideas is a form of community problem-solving, or advocacy. It is taking on new challenges, often by identifying a community need and documenting it, bringing together interested but possibly even disparate constituencies to solve the identified need. Sometimes the campaign is friendly and evokes smiling, upbeat, nice people; sometimes the campaign is motivated by pain and attracts emotion and those whose lives are characterized by far too much suffering. Some campaigns are driven by anger or angst. But there is plenty to do. What are you waiting for?

Alan Jennings, left, executive director of Community Action Committee of the Lehigh Valley, and Ryan Conrad, right, CEO of the Lehigh Valley Association of Realtors, discuss a study Tuesday finding whites and minorities were treated differently by real estate agents.

Copyright NJ Advance Media. All rights reserved. Reprinted with permission.

Chapter 18

Marx Was Wrong on at Least This Issue

I DON'T KNOW HOW MANY OF US HAVE READ OR WERE REQUIRED TO READ KARL MARX ANYMORE, AND BRINGING HIM UP IS DANGEROUS. But ignoring him is worse.

He had this theory called the historical dialectic. Abbreviated, the idea was that the forces of change come from movements, not the strength of leadership by great and/or charismatic and/or inspired and/or lucky people.

He called the status quo a mixture of culture, political economy, social structures and other forces the "thesis." Forces of change were called the "antithesis." In the struggle, sometimes revolutionary, the ensuing outcome of those countervailing forces was called the "synthesis."

Marx himself refuted the theory. So did Lenin. For that matter, so did Lennon. Then there's Hitler, many American presidents and European prime ministers. Some argue that Franklin Delano Roosevelt saved capitalism. Gandhi? MLK? Where would American domestic policy be without Ted Kennedy? My conservative friends would argue for including Reagan; that would be going too far. I'll trade you Lennon for Reagan.

BUT, IT'S REALLY ABOUT POWER

Why does this word bother you? Because Jesus said, "The meek shall inherit the earth?" That would be nice. The problem is that the powerful like their power and they aren't giving it up without a fight.

For some, the fight is a revolution. Not in this country. In the United States, the folks in power, especially the folks in power with money, are far too sophisticated. They'll give us a Roosevelt before they'll concede. He'll pacify the left, preserve capitalism and away we go. By the mid-1970's, income and wealth disparity were on a path back to being as bad as ever.

(And, besides, if there was a revolution in this country, I'm convinced it would come from the radical right. Folks on the left don't own guns. Folks on the right are mad as hell, they're well-armed, and they're dying to bust out their arsenals.)

Seek power. It is critical to your ability to change the world. Hopefully, this book will help.

THAT'S RIGHT, I SAID "SEEK POWER"

Look, if we are going to make change, we have to understand how power is accumulated and how to effectively use it. Much of this book, really, is about how to do just that. But let me throw out a few additional key points:

THIS IS PARTLY ABOUT LEADERSHIP

I'm not going to include any of those executive leadership how-to manuals that are popular with the self-help crowd. My advice is more raw.

Here it is:
- A leader is willing to work harder than anyone else in the organization;
- A leader has vision and communicates it effectively;
- A leader is inclusive, but should try to lead those s/he includes, not follow the popular perspective;
- A leader strives for perfection and demands it of those around him/her;
- A leader has thick skin but still cares enough about being hurt to listen to those around him/her;
- A leader is driven, obsessed;
- These days, in the nonprofit sector, a leader must be an entrepreneur;
- A leader understands how a "cult of personality" can be an effective weapon or it can cause mass destruction;
- A leader is smart enough to understand the multiplicity of forces that give a community some degree of uniqueness that could almost be characterized as a "personality," and how to affect, intervene in, if not manipulate it.

- There is nothing more powerful in the battle than integrity; and besides, we ain't got no money, so how else can we have credibility?
- Know what you are talking about and say it with confidence.
- Don't push so hard that you can't win, i.e. be reasonable.
- Too much swagger, too much bluster, too much arrogance will cost you everything, so don't be a jerk.

IMAGE-MAKING

OK, so I'm guilty of elevating the debate from one that got little attention to one that gets a lot. I'm guilty of making CACLV the premier advocate in the region and among the tops statewide. I'm guilty of being the one who prods, pricks, hounds, badgers the press on how and whether they cover poverty and its many implications. I'm guilty of letting my obsession with justice, my intensity, passion, anger, empathy, sympathy, impatience get the best of me.

You got a problem with that?

Along the way we have brought many, many groups and individuals along for the ride. We have made sure that those left out, those boxed in, those marginalized have had a role in the decision-making, a leadership role, and amplified their voices.

We have also built the capacity of this community through a variety of stakeholder groups to address issues that affect the quality of life beyond our own organization and the people we serve directly: We pushed the counties to create a revenue stream to fund affordable housing, generating millions over the life of the fund, a small fraction of which came to the agency I lead; we led the passage of two voter referenda that generated more than $60 million for open space and parks. We bugged the suburban municipalities to fund the region's homeless shelters, not just the shelters we ran. Our use of the Community Reinvestment Act resulted in upwards to $1 billion in community development resources.

You can call me a self-promoter. But that positioning has made a difference that goes well beyond any benefit to this organization. The trolls that comment on the blogs get their kicks out of calling me an egomaniac. Maybe. But the cause is just. The spoils are typically shared. And I haven't gotten any benefit other than the occasional sense that I've made a small difference.

I don't have a marketing background, but I have my own sense of hip. I am an avid observer of culture, people watcher, trend watcher, message monitor. I've watched people lie brilliantly. I've watched them speak the truth unconvincingly. I've paid careful attention to the music, art, dance. I've watched commercials with a critical eye. I've watched the polls, I've worked the polls. I've conducted polls.

Out of all of that comes a clear sense of what I want the agency to look like, the agenda it sets, the message it communicates.

THE LOOK

Looking hip isn't cheap. So, when you are cheap – CACLV cheap – you have to beg, borrow, steal. OK, really, when you're CACLV cheap, everything you do feels like you're begging, borrowing and stealing. I get that. But while everyone might agree that we should spend as much of our funds as possible on services, opinion would vary widely on how much money to spend, if any, on "marketing," whether it's reaching out to people who need you or it's jockeying for contributions. I'm the marketing department at CACLV. Just about every nonprofit of our size in the region has a "marketing" or "communications" staffer or even department.

AM I RETENTIVE, OBSESSIVE-COMPULSIVE OR JUST ANNOYINGLY NEUROTIC?

You should try to have consistency in the materials you generate. It will make you look professional, well-organized, on the same page, easier to recognize. Use the same font in all of your written materials. Formats on such things as letters, essays, memos, and position papers on policy issues also convey a well-trained staff. If people can spot CACLV before they scrutinize a document, we're on the right track.

IS THE DEMAND FOR PERFECTION REALLY THAT UNREASONABLE?

Typos on correspondence, position papers, proposals or any other documents that will find their way outside of the building are just unacceptable. What percentage error rate is acceptable? Well, let's look at Platinum Glove winner Manny Machado. The kid got the award for being the top defensive player in the American League at age 21. His fielding percentage strikes me as a fair comparison. In the year he got the award his fielding percentage was a stingy .973. That means out of every 1,000 fielding chances, he only made an error in 27. In a world where we have "spell-check" and "grammar-check," there really is no excuse for errors – they will both be trying to rat you out. Let's start thinking in terms of perfection. It's possible, you know.

THE ATTITUDE. THE MESSAGE.
CACLV is an agency with an attitude. I have a game face for my work-related news stories. Denise says I often look angry. I am angry. And I'm damned serious about the cause. I still have a lot of counter-cultural sense of humor about me. At the end of the day I have played the Flintstone's theme song ("Yabba Dabba Do!"), "Hi, Ho!" as sung by the Seven Dwarfs in Disney's "Snow White," and "It's a Five O'Clock World," by The Vogues over the PA system in our main office building in Bethlehem. I'll take on anyone at ping pong who thinks they can beat me. I sang back-up vocals with the band at our holiday party.

The ad agency that was doing our work for us can't break out of its corporate look. For the first draft of the first of our Annual Reports they'd done for us, they had a young mother joyfully running in a meadow on a sunny day with her three-year-old. I think there were even bluebirds in the picture. And daisies.

"What the hell is this?" My friend, the owner, must have known there was no way I would go with it. It might as well have been the album cover for "It's a Beautiful Day," by the band with the same name.

"Mike, come on. You were once a rebel. My world doesn't look like this picture. My world is gritty, sullen, and filled with despair. Let's get a look that says we have serious work to do and we all need to work on it together."

We get back together a week or two later. I think the butterflies might have been removed. Maybe even the daisies. But the sun was still shining. People were still happy.

Here's the message I want our look to convey:

Folks, we're damned serious about our work. We aren't going to waste a nickel or a minute knowing you're out there and things aren't going well. We will fight almost any battle if the cause is just.

We aren't going to present ourselves as happy, as if we can make all problems go away. We are going to present ourselves as determined, as cheap, as dissatisfied as long as someone is the victim of injustice. We won't be walking "on the sunny side of the street," as the song goes. We are more likely to be on the dark side, where people hang their heads low, where hope wanes, where opportunity is in short supply.

Chapter 19

Good Customer Service in an Era When "Good Customer Service" is an Oxymoron

IT MIGHT SOUND OLD-FASHIONED BUT WE ACTUALLY CARE ABOUT PEOPLE. When you leave our offices we want you to feel like you've never been treated better. (We have some work to do on that one.)

Good customer service includes dressing like a professional. Now, we have people who work in a warehouse and crawl around in attic crawl spaces. But even under those circumstances you can set a high standard for that particular situation.

It means that the voices on our end of the phone line sound like they're smiling when speaking. It means friendly but professional. It means prompt. And respectful.

Real people answer our phones. I hate it when phone calls automatically go to voice mail. Our people are hurting, they need answers; many are in crisis. Can't we do better than that?

We are open and available from 8 A.M. until 5 P.M. That's nine hours, not the standard eight. We made that move when welfare reform was passed and we knew that we needed to be available at least a little longer than a full-time worker's typical workday, since most poor people are working. It is maddening to need services and not be able to connect because of being employed.

We have a position on staff whose job is to put some effort into assisting people who call but we can't serve. Just about every agency has agonized over what to do with people who need help that they don't provide. So, what we all tend to do is refer the individual to the agency that might possibly on a sunny day if it's the second week of the month, maybe be able to help. We give them the phone number and, after hanging up, say a little prayer that we just did the right thing. Poor soul on the phone, though, is in referral purgatory.

WE DON'T DO ANYTHING FOR ANYONE
This is one of the fundamental points to be taken from this book:

Don't call me a bleeding heart; it's not a compliment. Bleeding hearts tend to be enablers, enablers tend to disempower people, disempowered people tend to accept their lot. When you accept your lot, you give up. When you give up, you think of yourself as a loser, often becoming depressed, getting stuck in both economic and emotional ruts from which you don't even care to escape, much less find motivation to try. You can bet you're passing on a life sentence of poverty and misery to your kids.

On top of it all, you're reinforcing what so many Americans think about poor people, leading voters to pick candidates who will deal harshly with "lazy welfare bums." Before you know it, our country's approach to poverty is barely an approach; it's a retreat, a full-blown, yellow-bellied, spineless denial of a civilized country's role in uplifting its most vulnerable. And innocent people, good people, young, old, men, women, white, black are denied the support needed to scratch out a better life.

This should be about teaching people how to fight their own battles, solve their own problems.

I don't even like the word, "help." It sounds pathetic. It sounds like, "you need me."

In fact, the whole notion of "human services" suggests you are the problem. You obviously don't see the endless opportunities to become a wealthy business owner in this great country of ours. Sit down, shut up, listen to your caseworker tell you how to make it work in America.

Some use the metaphorical "give a man a fish" admonition. Our way of making the point is this: We don't do anything for anyone. Like the attitude? We're an agency with an attitude.

So, we don't do anything for anyone.

OK, we do plenty. But I hope you get the point. The question is, how do we operationalize that attitude?

The Sixth Street Shelter is our short-term (60 days) transitional housing program for homeless families with children. It is the largest shelter for families in the region, perhaps in eastern Pennsylvania. There are 25 apartments; each family that stays at the Sixth Street Shelter has its own fully-equipped apartment. No sharing kitchens or bathrooms with complete strangers. The building is, without question, the nicest property in the neighborhood. It's what a shelter run by a community development organization looks like.

Here's the deal: Just like so much of society, we have (or should have) obligations to each other. Our obligation to you is to provide you with a decent place to live, the compassionate and empowering support of our staff, assistance in finding an appropriate and affordable permanent place to live, and follow-up support for a year after you leave.

Your obligation to yourself, your family and the community that was there when you needed it is to play by the rules, which includes keeping your apartment clean and neat (we inspect weekly), respecting your neighbors as it relates to noise, no smoking, drinking, weapons or drugs, no guests, and young children may not be left alone. In addition, you will be obligated to pay, if possible, up to $25 per week and to save 50 percent of the balance of any income you might have (this is essential to being able to exit, since tenants will need a security deposit and first month's rent). Perhaps most importantly, you will have to identify the issues that complicate your life and resulted in your homelessness and must be addressed, if not resolved. This means developing a goal plan for stabilizing your crisis and getting on track to become more financially self-sufficient.

Your counselor is there to lead you when you are lost, support you when you stumble, cheer you on when you're down, help you up when you fall. Get up, stiffen your lip, dig down deep for new motivation and resolve.

We can't help you if you won't help yourself. The roof over your head or the bed when you're weary are not going to make the difference in your life. Only you can make that difference and when it becomes apparent that you lack the will, we will ask you to leave. At any given time there are 50 to 100 families on our waiting list and there aren't enough resources in our community to support those who expect someone else to solve all their problems. If you are prepared to blow the opportunity we are providing you, then we will make room for the family that is waiting, hoping, perhaps praying for the opportunity you appear willing to blow.

Sounds rough, I know. Some call it tough love. Some think of it as a conservative approach. I think it is empowering insofar as it places faith in you to muster the will to pick yourself up, dust yourself off and get back in the game. If you leave our care without learning how to solve your own problems, we have failed.

All we can really accomplish in a 60-day shelter is stabilizing the crisis and getting people headed in the right direction. Those who are especially motivated to move on have an opportunity to take advantage of our long-term transitional housing programs at Turner Street Apartments in downtown Allentown or Ferry Street Apartments in Easton. There, we up the proverbial ante, giving our families two years to make a much more complete transition to greater financial self-sufficiency by participating in any number of vocational readiness programs, whether they be English as a Second Language, GED, job training or even college.

Photograph courtesy of Keenan-Nagle Advertising, Inc.

Section III

The Long and Really Winding Road

Chapter 20

They Fight Poverty, Don't They?

WE MIGHT THINK SO. BUT OUR APPROACH IS FLAWED.

THE HUMAN SERVICES MODEL
The thinking here is that you're the problem. Not you, but you, the person who is poor. Sit down, shut up and listen to your book-educated caseworker tell you how, if you just embraced his or her approach, you will be fine. Can't be the system, you know. So what if most poor people work? It's still your fault.

The problem is that if we pulled off a miracle with every family that went through our transitional housing programs, stabilized their crisis, put them on the right track, got them job training or more education but they had no choice but to move into a neighborhood where there aren't any jobs, the buses don't take them where the jobs are located, they can't find quality child care, the housing is substandard and unaffordable, the streets aren't safe and the schools struggle to teach, that miracle won't stick.

So this effort of ours to save the world is really about economic opportunity.

How can someone think about their career goals when they are not sure where their next meal will come from or whether they will lose their home to eviction due to failure to afford their rent?

HELPING THE WINNERS GET OUT, LEAVING THE LOSERS BEHIND
The other flawed model is the idea that all we need to do is get you (again, you, the poor person) out of the ghetto. First, it ain't easy to get someone out, given the cost of housing outside of the ghetto, zoning restrictions and other forms of racism and classism that are designed to exclude folks. But, if we help the "winners" get out and leave the proverbial "losers" behind, we are conceding the permanent ghetto. And in many low-income neighborhoods, the peer pressure is to fail, not succeed.

The much better strategy would be to transform our neighborhoods into places that offer a better quality of life, one that is appealing enough to those who can afford to get out but, instead, choose to stay. In order to have a functional neighborhood, you need a functional marketplace. And you can't have a functional marketplace where everyone is poor.

OK, sure, start yapping about gentrification. This anti-poverty activist is not anti-gentrification. There. I said it. Again.

Chapter 21

How the Mainstream Media Work and How You Can Use It for the Cause

IF YOU ARE IN THE NEWS BUSINESS AND EVERYONE HATES YOU, YOU'RE DOING YOUR JOB PROPERLY. Of course, it's better if everyone loves you, but that ain't gonna happen. So, you'll take what you can get. Everyone hates you.

The wacky right, though, hated the mainstream media for reporting on how wacky the wacky right was. Enter Fox News. Leave it to horse's ass Roger Ailes to hook up with Rupert Murdoch and do far better at showing their true colors than the mainstream media ever did; the fact is, Fox "News" is the official news outlet of the kooky right. So, the wacky right wing hates all of the media except Fox. The rest of us hate Fox.

The good news is, most of us will never deal with the media at the national level. The traditional rules of the press still apply to most of us operating at the local level. And that's a good thing. Because if you understand the rules, see the power in the press and are willing to use it, you can make a ton of change in your community.

One thing folks don't seem to understand is that what we do is news. Declining homeownership, rising rents are news. Wages not keeping up with inflation with conservatives blocking a minimum wage increase is news. A local nonprofit turning people away because of budget cuts is news. School performance disparities between urban and suburban school districts is news. For whatever reason, though, we don't deliver it to those who report it in a way that makes it news.

So, stick with me; this is a skill that you must deploy effectively if you are going to be a change agent. It will improve your fundraising and volunteer recruitment, and increase your power as politicians and other leaders realize you're capable of making lives better or worse depending on whether they do the right thing.

LET'S START WITH THE MECHANICS

The Desk
Also known as the assignment editor, the Desk is where the most important decisions get made. The assignment editor knows what "the budget" (how much room is available for stories) is for the next paper; it depends, largely, on the amount of advertising that has been sold. She (I'm using the feminine gender because my favorites are women) has an accumulation of media advisories (announcements of news events the vast array of "special" interests have cooked up for that day and are jockeying for attention, hoping they will be covered). Then, real news happens throughout the day – fires, crashes, politicians who do stupid things, businesses that get busted for putting profits ahead of the common good. The person at the Desk has to make the decisions on what gets covered, what doesn't.

Reporters
Some reporters have "beats," topical areas that reporters are assigned, like the city beat, the crime beat, the county beat, the arts and culture beat, business. Others are stuck in a news netherworld of having to wait for an assignment. A lot of reporters hate that – they get stuck having to write about the weather, the prominent community leader who died, final shopping day before Christmas or the latest Eagle Scout project.

Try to have a reporter in your Rolodex (or whatever the name of today's high-tech alternative is) who you know is interested in your issues and include him/her in the announcement. This person might nag the desk about getting that assignment and strengthen the likelihood the issue you are peddling gets the attention it deserves.

The Big Guy
The top dog in a newsroom is the managing editor or executive editor. This guy (right gender, unfortunately, despite progress that has been made) is the big picture guy. He and his assistant managing editors "budget" the available space I mentioned above. They decide what stories get how much room, where they're placed, whether there are any thematic subjects that include sidebars (story off-shoots) and other complementary stories, how a story is going to be played given the many angles.

You don't, typically, talk to these guys. They're largely inaccessible.

The Publisher
The publisher runs the business. People don't believe this, but the publisher generally stays out of the newsroom lest s/he wants to find him- or herself facing a mutiny from reporters, the desk, the managing editor and the assistant managing editors.

When you see the publisher, be friendly, reintroduce yourself, tell him or her how well the paper seems to be doing and keep moving right along.

ORGANIZING A MEDIA EVENT
You think you have a story worthy of press coverage. Are you sure it's worthy? Holding an event that wastes the press's time because it really wasn't newsworthy is a sure bet to cost you credibility the next time you organize an event.

So, you have an announcement that you really think has news value. There are standard ways to do this: I call it the choreography of the event.

Let's say you are buying a bigger warehouse out of which to operate your regional food bank. First, pick a venue. Keep in mind that you want pictures: not only do they paint a thousand words, but they attract attention to your story. It makes perfect sense to make the announcement at the new facility. Not so fast. Maybe you want to announce that you have put your current facility on the market. Hold the event amidst those stacks of pallets of food in the inadequate existing building. Get a second news hit for your food bank by holding a second announcement at the building you have now got under agreement to purchase.

David Erdman recently retired as long-time top guy at The Morning Call, the daily with the third-highest circulation in Pennsylvania. Dave and I practically grew up together, me as source and newsmaker, he as reporter, editor and, shortly before his retirement, publisher.

Dave confirms my opinion that holding an event late in the morning, say, around 10 or 11 a.m., "is ideal because you will benefit from an entire day or more of website play and broadcast play and also take advantage of the social media cycles. This way you will benefit from website and social media consumption spikes at noon. If for logistical purposes you must hold your announcement later in the day, keep in mind that another social media consumption spike happens in the evening hours, after 8 p.m.

"In addition to understanding deadlines for print and broadcast times, it is also good to understand how the outlet presents coverage on their website. This will help you to tailor your announcement planning to give a nod to video, graphics and other visual elements you might provide or facilitate for the reporter."

Dave knows his stuff and I am famously stupid when it comes to technology, so I have little to offer on the use of social media. We do use Facebook and a blog but I wouldn't claim to have a lot to offer on their highest and best uses.

For speakers, you have a variety of forces in play. Think about what you need, short- and long-term, when organizing a media event. Whose attention and/or support do you need? What prospective donors do you need if you're going to be effective raising the money to pay for it? Are there politicians with whom you could use a stronger relationship? Is it OK for all the participants to be white men (that's a rhetorical question)? How will you illustrate the breadth and depth of the need? Your board president probably should have a role. What else? You know better than I do what your institutional needs are.

> **HERE IS WHAT THE CHOREOGRAPHY MIGHT LOOK LIKE:**
>
> **Board president** — Emcees the event and makes announcement
>
> **Unemployed person** — Describes the need in human terms
>
> **Chair of task force** — Describes challenges of the inadequately-sized building and the need for a bigger building
>
> **Member of Congress** — Explains political realities in D.C. and how the need for food banks isn't going away
>
> And these events really shouldn't be more than 40 minutes at the absolute most – 20 or 30 minutes is better.

Do you see the manipulation? Er, I'm sorry, I meant, do you see how the choices for the event are designed to address other motives? They go beyond the simple announcement and set up the project, connect the problem to key people, make fighting poverty a mainstream issue, comment on the public policy issues that are left, unaddressed and, consequently, causing more need for the local community to get involved.

Getting the Press to Cover It
This is the role of the media advisory. The media advisory is an announcement directed to the press of an event they should cover. It is written like a news story but only provides the very basic information, including the "what, where, when and why" of the event. The "what" should include just enough information to get their attention but not so much that they don't need to cover it because they got the story from the advisory.

The typical media advisory would have, at the top, when the advisory can be put into play, which can be anytime between when it is received ("For Immediate Release") and when the event begins ("Please Embargo Until the Scheduled Event").

The advisory should have a headline. The body of the advisory would start with a "who, what, where, when" first paragraph. The second paragraph might have some information on the event without divulging too much detail. This is important. If they can get their story out of the advisory they are less likely to actually cover the event and, in the process, miss key additional information and photo opportunities that get more readers' attention. The final paragraph should be a description of the sponsoring organization.

A sample of such an advisory is in the appendix.

The advisory should go to the desk and to a reporter who you know cares about your issues.

Send it to the news media no more than three days before the event. Also, it is very important that you make follow-up calls. Your only intent, at least as you explain it to the newsroom, is to make sure they got the advisory. Call both the desk and your favored reporter. But do not, and the emphasis is important, do not ask them if they plan to cover it. That sounds like you're asking them for a favor. You don't want favors – if a reporter thinks they helped you, essentially overstepping the line on objectivity, they may try to take back that favor in how they cover the event. You never know.

The Press Release
The press release has a couple purposes: first, it is sent to the news outlets that were sent the advisory but did not, for whatever reasons, cover the event. Send it sometime around when the event is taking place, typically, between one hour prior to the scheduled event and two hours after it concludes. Hopefully, some of those outlets will run the story off the press release. The second purpose of the release is to hand it out at the event with the hope that it will ensure the facts were correct as they were written down by the reporters present.

A press release should be written as if it were the news article itself. Write it the way you wish the media was covering it, presenting it using objective language, providing quotes from the individuals who participate in the press conference, and as many of the facts as possible. The intent here is to minimize human error. A sample from an actual news event we conducted can be found in the appendix.

THE PRESS PACKET
This is an important tool for the event. It ensures the reporters covering the story get the facts straight. It ensures names are spelled correctly. The press packet should include the following:

- An agenda (this provides accurately-spelled names, titles and affiliation for each of the speakers);

- The aforementioned press release;

- Any supporting information that might be helpful, such as a fact sheet on local hunger and poverty or information on the program or the agency that runs it;

- The business card of the key contact in case the reporter has additional questions when s/he returns to the newsroom.

You should have enough copies to provide one to each reporter as well as extra copies that those in attendance might want to have.

Miscellaneous Things to Consider

Choose a venue that has symbolic value or makes for a picturesque backdrop. Make sure the venue does not have noise challenges (for example, a loud HVAC system that would make distracting ambient noise) or other issues (for example, it is accessible for people with disabilities). Be sure there is a podium that can handle mics used by radio or television news and a public address system so that those in attendance can hear the announcement.

Hang a sign or banner with the agency's name and logo in plain view in a prominent location -- for example, behind the podium -- so that any photos or film will pick up the name of your organization.

Make sure all printed material is typed in the same font (otherwise, it will make your organization look scattered).

When news articles appear, get copies. Those articles can be useful for grant proposals and promotional materials. If nothing else, they're good for posterity or for sending five copies to your mother.

Line up someone, or maybe several someones, to write letters to the editor praising your event.

Do not thank the reporters or editors or anyone else in the news organization. They did their jobs. Your thanks might be interpreted as, "Wow! You guys made us look really great!" (See the paragraph above telling you not to get too cozy; they'll jilt you in a heartbeat.)

On the agenda, end it with Q&A. Don't expect any, though. My experience is that the reporters will want to speak with you privately so that their competition does not get the benefit of their brilliantly insightful questions.

Make sure each speaker knows what you expect them to cover. You might want to provide "talking points" for each speaker so they cover everything thoroughly, emphasize key common points, stay on message and make the points in the language the organization typically uses.

OTHER TRICKS OF THE TRADE
You should be constantly thinking about how you can influence the flow of information to your community through the news media. After all, there is no downside to press coverage (assuming you're not an idiot).

Be helpful. When you hear of newsworthy developments, let your contacts know. There is no way they won't feel at least a little indebted to you. Maybe they'll even behave like human beings and feel guilty if they ever make you look bad. Know as much about your community as possible so they begin to see you as a resource well beyond your specific field of influence.

SHOOT FOR THE BOLD QUOTE
Most print media these days will pull the most powerful, most thoughtful or most idiotic quote that encapsulates best the point of the story and increase the

font size, make it bold and put it in a shaded box. This, of course, makes it more likely to be read.

Most people have a pattern for how they race through the paper, or scan through their digital news feed, given being in a morning hurry. They'll read the headline, probably, too, the subheadings that are seen in most articles these days. If there is a bold quote, that is likely to be read, as are the captions with some photos. So, your goal should be to shoot for that bold quote. My friend, David Erdman, former editor-in-chief at The Morning Call, the largest daily in the region, says this: If there is supplementary information such as data that the reporter can build into a graphic, this can add to the media outlet's digital presentation and mean better exposure for you. Any renderings or other visuals also will enhance the digital display you receive; be sure to provide any images on a thumb drive or email them to the reporter at high resolution.

DON'T GET CAUGHT OFF-GUARD
Not that quick on the draw? Do this: When a reporter calls you and asks if you have a minute to talk, ask them if you can call them right back, certainly within 10 minutes. If they say "no," take the call and take your chances. If they agree, ask them what they're calling about. Then spend the next couple minutes coming up with some zingers and call them back.

I'm pretty sure I lead the league in those quotes. When the paper did a New Year's feature on the top quotes of the year, I'm there. When the paper runs their Sunday feature quote of the week, I'll get in there once or twice each year. Not bragging – I'm just making sure you know the possibilities. Surely you can understand the benefits of being used in the press so frequently.

The power of the press may be weakened but, short of buying big-time advertisements, it is a very effective strategy for making a difference, as your voice and the opinions you express carry much greater weight.

MAKE SURE YOU KNOW WHAT "OFF THE RECORD" MEANS
Most people who watch but do not create news think "off the record" means the reporter cannot use what the source/newsmaker is about to say (one should always state something is off the record before one says it). The reporter can use it but be

sure to negotiate this clearly with the reporter and specify what you mean. The more precise term for this type of use is "not for attribution," meaning you are providing the information but it is not to be tied back to you; you are not to be named as the source. They can quote the comment and cite the source without naming names. For example, the reporter could say, "According to a prominent local activist..." and lots of people will figure the reporter is talking about you. Or, the reporter could take the comment to another source, who could substantiate it and to whom it could be attributed. The safest thing to do is not make the comment in the first place. However, in my world of manipulation, er, sorry, I meant, in my world of using a variety of means to persuade people to do things they wouldn't do if I weren't bugging them, confidentiality can be powerful: it can redirect a story, expose someone, push someone to divulge something they had no intention of divulging.

My advice is that you try not to use the jargon. Instead, explain to the reporter how s/he can use what you said. Being careless with what you think are off-the-record comments can really get you burned. So again, be very clear with the reporter exactly what you mean.

I have gone this far: I gave a reporter what I knew was confidential information that my source probably didn't want me to give them. I told the reporter they could not use it, that I would deny ever saying it and would never be available as a source again if s/he used it in any way. That was pretty clear (actually, I might have even added that I'd have to kill them and use the mulcher that was used in "Fargo" to dispose of their body).

So, you wonder, why give them information under those terms? Again, the manipulator in me has motives. I may want them to chase a story that I don't have time to pursue. I would allow them, if they found anyone else who could corroborate the story, to come back to me for possible comment or additional information. That results in the story finding its way into the public realm and ensures that we get in the story. There are plenty of situations where these subtleties are useful.

Ultimately, a good reporter needs good sources. Be one. They will make sure to protect you as a resource. Remember: we are all human, need each other in one way or another, and will protect our relationships because they are important to us.

ON COZINESS

A good reporter will never let you get too cozy – they know it will compromise their independence and their obsession with objectivity. You don't need much coziness; you just want a productive relationship with a key vehicle to accumulating influence.

You also want to have a productive relationship with more than one reporter at each news outlet. Reporters don't stick around long – they move on to bigger outlets in bigger markets, they move up into editorial or management positions, they get downsized. Losing your one and only news contact means starting over.

When you really gain serious respect from reporters, they'll call you periodically just to ask if you have any stories for them. Don't pass up that pay-off for your hard work!

Copyright NJ Advance Media. All rights reserved. Reprinted with permission.

Chapter 22

Taking on a Consensus Bad Guy: The Slum Landlord

IT HAPPENS LIKE THIS

In most regions, it is the older communities where the problem begins. They tended to get their start near some kind of natural geological feature that attracts commerce. It could be a waterway that enabled goods to be moved quickly to market. It could be some kind of mineral deposit, like shale or slate or limestone or coal. Communities popped up around that industry. High-density, low-cost housing would be built within walking distance; the folks with access to transportation built their homes at some distance from the riff raff, the ethnic groups those very same companies often seduced to come to America to provide a cheap source of labor. Merchants set up shop nearby and soon there was a business district or "downtown."

Eventually, access to transportation became more universal, first with trolleys, then the automobile. As workers eventually won various battles, and gained the means they moved out, making room in that high-density, low-cost housing they once called home. Highways developed and those people of means crafted a very effective tool to keep those who didn't look like them or sound like them out. Land use planning, or zoning, as it is also called, became the trick for segregating people. New schools would be built that were bigger, more comfortable, newer than the ones left behind. There was a natural flow of capital out of the older communities into the newer ones. Those fortunate enough to be allowed in could afford services but didn't need them. Those unfortunate enough to be left behind needed the services but couldn't afford them.

Those older municipalities would have two options for dealing with the ever increasing cost of services: They could raise taxes, chasing out those who could afford to get out; or they could cut services, diminishing the quality of life and chasing out those who could afford to get out. The tax base dwindled, making the cost of compensating for those changes even greater.

In a normal, market-driven world, you get what you pay for: If you can't afford a Mercedes, you buy a Honda. However, in this new, more segregated America, that formula was turned on its head. The higher the quality of life, typically the less (in taxes) you would pay for it. To add insult to the injury, the folks who set the table so effectively would wag their fingers and tsk tsk at those whose communities were rotting.

As the people with the money fled, they often found it difficult to sell their house. Along came investors smart enough to spot a market opportunity. These investors bought those homes and subdivided them into multiple rental units. The result would be doubling or tripling the density, bringing a doubling or tripling of the problems with it. The quality of life slips further, pushing more out. Left behind are schools without a tax base, aging infrastructure without a tax base, police and fire protection without a tax base.

Here in the Lehigh Valley, the Lehigh Valley Planning Commission pointed out that between 1991 and 2006, the tax base of the three cities rose by just .5 percent while the tax base of our suburban townships rose more than 51 percent. Do the math – the disparity is a factor of 100. Under these circumstances, urban communities are unsustainable. Scumbags do their best work in aberrant marketplaces. Enter the slum landlords. I'm not talking about the people who become landlords by default because they couldn't sell their house. I'm talking about those who exploit the margins of our marketplace and our society. They will whine and claim it's the tenants, those unwashed masses. True enough, if people on the margins behaved more responsibly this equation wouldn't work so well for the predators. On the other hand, if the predators didn't exist, maybe more responsible landlords wouldn't tolerate the tenants' bull shit. In either case, the municipality is left dealing with both sides of the equation with minimal tax base to pay for it.

And it just feeds on itself.

We thought it was about time we took this one on. We opened more than one front on the issue.

Thanks to the VISTA program, we had a community organizer, a Latino kid out of Jersey who was attending Muhlenberg College, here in Allentown.

We did "drive-by," actually, walk-by observations of residential properties in the neighborhood surrounding the central business district. It's pretty safe to assume that, if a property looks like a dump from the street, the inside of the house is probably worse.

Our organizer would knock on doors at the properties that concerned us. He would tell the occupants what we were doing and they would let him in. It helped that he was a young adult Latino and not a white guy like me.

If the property was in poor enough condition we would encourage the tenant to file a complaint with the city code enforcement officer. We would then go to the county office of the recorder of deeds and mortgages to determine what other properties that particular landlord owned. While we were checking for ownership information we would also identify the source of the loan the investor had.

Not surprisingly, one of Allentown's most notorious slum landlord popped up right at the beginning. We will call this landlord "X". As we continued to walk the neighborhood, identifying problem properties, we continued to develop some solid data on property owners, which landlords were most apt to join a fight when we picked it and which banks are providing the capital for X and his understudies to ruin our neighborhoods.

A few banks were identified as possibly guilty parties but it didn't take us long to zero in on one in particular. We informed those few banks that we would be watching their lending practices as it relates to slum landlords buying more properties on which to prey. In the case of the bank that appeared to be the lender of choice for Allentown slum landlords, we paid a visit.

I told the bank's senior exec in charge of commercial lending that we were making a courtesy call to let them know that we were watching. We made sure they knew the conditions they were fostering and showed them pictures of the deals they facilitated, pointing out that their collateral might not be worth as much as they had hoped. We parted ways; I'm pretty sure we were clear about our agenda and that they understood what to expect from us.

We then began to organize a media event to attract attention to what a handful of creeps could do to a neighborhood's housing stock.

The neighborhood where we were focusing our attention was immediately adjacent to the central business district. The housing stock was loaded with older row houses typical of such communities, many of which were lovingly and tastefully rehabilitated. Within this neighborhood was a 22-square-block area known as Old Allentown, where many of the homeowners organized the Old Allentown Preservation Association (OAPA). This group and its activities were a key hedge against the march of blight in the downtown neighborhoods.

Among the activities organized by OAPA was an annual "house tour" that took place in October, designed to show prospective homebuyers how beautiful their homes could be. The tour was a popular event and well-known to Allentown area residents.

We decided to do a "Slum Tour." That got people's attention.

We identified about 10 properties that were worthy of inclusion due to the extent of the disrepair. We also considered whether the property was an aberration among the owner's properties or an illustration of the practice and pattern of the owner. They were all within walking distance of each other and their occupants were agreeable and, in some cases, enthusiastic about participating.

The idea was that we would lead a tour of the properties for reporters and various city and elected officials. When we arrived, the tenant would welcome the entourage and actually conduct the tour.

When we announced the event it was clear we had struck a nerve, generating a lot of chatter. One individual who was particularly angered by the event was the mayor. He huffed and puffed, criticizing the event, claiming there were no slums in our fair city. Those claims brought even more attention to the event, including ridicule by editorial writers. We had, indeed, struck a nerve.

The day of the event came and we gathered at the appointed time and place. We explained how the event would work and realized that the mayor had joined us. This should be fun. Like a Vanna White, "here is the faucet in the bathtub that doesn't work. Over here you'll find flaking lead paint. Overhead is the discolored ceiling that is proof of a roof leak we've been complaining about since we moved in more than a year ago. When I open this cabinet you'll see a bunch of our six-legged squatters scatter."

It all went as planned and the media did its job. We had successfully placed a new issue on the community problem-solving agenda for the city. And the mayor looked foolish arguing with us.

One of the things we learned from this campaign was that the city's code enforcement office was so understaffed that, when an inspection was conducted and code violations identified, the inspectors could not follow up to determine whether or not the work was done. It doesn't take the bad guys long to figure that out.

We proposed an ordinance that would raise fees on all rental units except those owned by the Allentown Housing Authority. Those fees would fund additional inspectors who would now systematically inspect all rental units at least once every five years. (Until then, inspections were only conducted when a complaint was filed.)

Not long after the event we learned that some of the block watches in the city were interested in the same issue that we were. Those groups were dominated by homeowners while our effort was focused on poor people. They toiled in pursuit of their perspective while we toiled in pursuit of ours. They thought they were on to something but we had stolen the attention. We knew how difficult it was to organize poor people and that we needed them to get anything accomplished. We joined forces.

The block watches wanted another key component added to the campaign. They were sick of the quality of life in their neighborhoods being disrupted by noisy, disrespectful, bad asses. They wanted a mechanism for dealing with it. The outcome was a proposal for a "disruptive conduct behavior" provision. People who violated neighbors' quality of life would be cited. Three citations in a 12-month period would result in a mandatory eviction. Because some people worried that this provision would be used to target people of color, an appeal process would be included as part of that provision.

We took our proposal to City Council. Now, you would have to know the cast of characters in this group. Maybe communities all across the country have this sort of mix. If so, no wonder our cities can't find a way to get back in business. In Allentown, we have what I call the Stupid Caucus. It always seems to find a way to get one of their own elected. In our case, we had a nasty little woman named Emma Tropiano. She would say things like, "99 percent of the crime being committed in this city is committed by Hispanics." Or, "all the Puerto Ricans ever do is sit on their front porch waiting for their welfare check." Yikes.

Mrs. Tropiano would then be the lead vote-getter in the next election. I'm not kidding.

The New York Times Magazine ran a feature story entitled "The Latinization of Allentown." Mrs. Tropiano was all over that article. I made a point of pushing back. As you can imagine, this got people's attention. Now I'm being interviewed on Swiss television about racism in Allentown, Pennsylvania, in the good ol' USA.

Mrs. Tropiano and I became mortal enemies. She once made a comment that I thought I was Allentown's own Jesus Christ. Nice gal.

Mrs. Tropiano was a slum landlord. And, because she felt that most of the problems were being caused by Latinos there was no need to do anything to improve the quality of life of those people. She fought us.

Allentown had made changes to its charter recently that required a super-majority of the seven-member Council to approve a tax increase. With the slum landlord leading the way, we could only muster four of the five votes we needed. So we launched a campaign to force the city to adopt our initiative through a voter referendum.

We had a ball.

The campaign we ran was pretty damned brilliant, if I must say so myself. We had a poster child for the campaign. No, it wasn't X. It appeared to us that X was bringing along a coterie of X wannabes and the poster child was one of them. We used the poster child over and over again: We held a press conference in front of his properties, used photos of his properties in our printed material and took his name in vain. That poor bastard must have been a member of the Stupid Caucus, because he kept doing more stupid things.

The referendum passed by a vote of 85 percent to 15 percent. This is flat out remarkable. If we were to hold a referendum on the question of whether the sun rose from the East I'm not sure we could get 85 percent of that vote, especially considering the presence of the Stupid Caucus. The project got the attention of other communities in our region and beyond. I think at least a dozen communities have copied our ordinance.

A year after our courtesy call on the slum landlords' lender of choice, we called again. I had had a student intern look at the mortgage filings in Allentown since our first visit. Sure enough, they had made seven new loans. We scheduled an appointment.

This time the CEO participated. Oddly enough, they had invited an examiner from the Federal Deposit Insurance Corporation. The CEO was pissed, insisting that I had gotten my facts wrong. At one point he was so angry, he was on his feet yelling at me. He was trying to take his blazer off and, because he was so fired up, was having difficulty, finally inverting the sleeves, then throwing the blazer at the couch in their board room.

"Let's invite [X] to join us."

OK, I say.

Within just a few minutes, X was there with us. It was obvious he had been waiting down the hall.

This was the first time we had met despite having an acrimonious relationship at a distance. I introduced myself. He said, "I know who you are. I've done my research on you. I know you went to Emmaus High School in the mid-1970s. And I know other things you wouldn't want to become public."

I said, "Let's get it out. And you better be damn sure you have your facts straight."

The CEO turned to X and said, "[X], how many loans have we made to you in the past year?"

"None."

"You see? You don't have your facts straight, Mr. Jennings. You didn't do your homework."

"Shit," I thought to myself. "Did my intern get it wrong?"

We parted. I thought I better get that information right. So, I went to the county office and looked in the records myself. There they were – seven new loans, two to X's wife and five to one of two shell companies he used. Those sons of bitches.

I called the head of commercial lending. "Mike, you said you didn't make any more loans to X. The record shows, and I did it myself, that you made two loans to his wife and five to his company."

"That's not X."

I couldn't believe how dishonest they could be.

So, my friends, not all lending in poor neighborhoods is a good thing. Keep an eye on the bastards.

Chapter 23

I Wish I'd Made This Up

THE ISSUE – THE INCIDENT – THAT ILLUSTRATES ALMOST EVERY POINT IN THIS BOOK WAS THE BATTLE – NO, THE WAR – THAT TOOK PLACE OVER THE HEART AND SOUL AND CONSCIENCE OF THE AMERICAN AND EVEN INTERNATIONAL FINANCIAL SECTOR SPILLING OVER INTO EVERY OTHER ASPECT OF OUR LIVES. We thought when the great guru, Federal Reserve Chairman Alan Greenspan began using the highly charged phrase "predatory lending" in reference to a massive crime being committed right in front of everybody, penetrating most homes and destroying countless financial lives that it would all be over, tout suite. Certainly, if the behavior was, indeed, predatory (in other words, abusive but focused on specific targets in the marketplace) then Chairman Greenspan would move swiftly to stop it if, for no other reason, but to protect his legacy.

If only.

Instead, I was sitting in the imposing and impressive Board of Governors room in a meeting with the chairman himself as part of the delegation of community development activists around the country who were members of the board of directors of the National Community Reinvestment Coalition and seeking the Fed's intervention. I heard the chairman call himself a "libertarian when it comes to access to credit. The market will work itself out." The man whose entire raison d'être on this planet is to intervene in the marketplace didn't want to intervene in the marketplace.

True enough. Shockingly so. The market completely collapsed, from Wall Street to Main Street to every street. And it didn't have to be that way. This is the story that pushes every button.

Stay with me.

PLUGGING IN
We got pretty good at expanding access to credit – mortgages, in particular – for homebuyers who historically were left out of the market. Spurred on by the Community Reinvestment Act, but still well within reasonable credit standards, people of color, single heads of household, lower-income households were getting mortgages. And keeping them.

In our home ownership counseling seminars, we told our participants that getting a subprime loan was God's way of telling you you weren't ready to buy a home. Stop. Save some money. Improve your credit score. Then buy a home you can afford. When the foreclosure crisis came years later very few of the people who were coming to us for help in rescuing their home had attended our seminars. Those who did were not losing their homes.

Unfortunately, a bunch of creeps running some obscure thrifts in southern California figured out that lots of people were being advised that way. Might as well rip them off. So, armies of mortgage brokers were dispatched to communities to find those people we were sending away and offer them a financing opportunity that will contradict our advice. It wasn't a coincidence that large numbers of victims of predatory lending were people of color, moderate-income people, and single-parent households.

The products they were peddling were called "high cost" loans and had interest rates double or more what people with responsible credit were paying. They had home equity loans that often stripped wealth right out of the pockets of the homeowners. They had "Liar Loans" (that's what we called them; the industry euphemistically called them "stated income" loans) that required, basically, no proof of anything. And they had "option ARMs," a particularly heinous product.

On top of that there was a veritable bacchanalia of unscrupulous, creepy people with no conscience getting fatter in every metaphorical sense of the word committing fraud just to add icing to the toxic cake.

Here in the Lehigh Valley, a very effective coalition of allied groups had just come off a big victory passing a referendum creating the apartment licensing initiative. Because of that campaign we had a lot of intelligence on many of the bad guys in the Allentown real estate market. Believe me: I'm telling you the abbreviated version of this sordid story. Because some pretty nasty tricks were being played in communities around the country we were watching carefully for signs of the same activity occurring here.

One key development was a phone call from a friend who ran a title insurance company and was a volunteer in our home ownership counseling program. She told me about a scheme she was watching in which investors were buying property at tax sale and flipping it at greatly inflated prices within days or even hours of the initial purchase. How could the house bought at sheriff sale for $27,000 sell just an hour later for $70,000? But more incredibly the investor wanted to sell the house before he bought it; my friend declined. But she wrote down the addresses of the properties and watched them. Just a few months later they turned up as distressed property owners. Again.

She called me to tell me about what she was observing and encouraged me to tackle it. Here's another reason to jump out of bed and race to work.

I did what I have often done: I took the story to a local newspaper. It took a while but they did an outstanding job. They identified a local appraiser who had been watching the same transactions and found the key piece of the puzzle – the appraisers. She ratted one out. The rogue appraiser was given a slap on the wrist: $1,000 fine and probation for one year, during which the appraiser could still do business but would agree to random checks on his business.

With the newspaper article published, clearly showing illegal behavior, we sat back and waited for the guys in the white hats to ride into town and haul the bad asses away. We waited. We tapped our feet, we watched the clock. We waited, chins in hand. And we waited. Nothing.

Then came another key development. One of my employees who speaks Spanish was dispatched to go talk to the owner of a house in one of the distressed neighborhoods in Center City. He showed me his settlement sheet from closing on his house. It was dripping with fraud. It showed that he had made a down payment. He says he didn't have any money. It showed that his wages were adequate to afford his monthly payments; they weren't. It showed that he paid $67,000 for the house but there is no way a legitimate appraisal would have come to that conclusion. It showed he had a bankable credit score; he said there was no way.

As part of the bird-dogging of properties being done by a city employee during the apartment licensing campaign, we were able to get very interesting information about who was buying properties, where they were being bought, who was selling them and more. And these guys were brazen. A couple dozen properties were flipped within days or even on the same day they were bought, with no time to make the kind of improvements that would justify doubling or even tripling the price. The article explained the property flipping and its reliance on complicit appraisers. In plain view, then, the flipping continued.

I was determined to get these sons of bitches.

Armed with the data from the property flipping I went knocking on doors. In most cases the person answering the door was a woman of color, usually Latina, almost always looking at me with that look of suspicion on her face. Who is this white guy in a suit knocking on my door in the evening?

"Hi. I'm Alan Jennings and I work for the Community Action Committee of the Lehigh Valley. I understand you paid $67,000 for your house."

There's that suspicious look. I'm guessing she didn't know that the sale price of her house is public information.

"You realize that the guy who sold it to you only paid $23,000 for it?" That question was usually met with a look of surprise, sometimes horror. "Are you happy with the improvements that were made?"

Her response was often something along the lines of, "Are you serious?! Come in and take a look at this place!"

Now I'm in the house.

"Here's the faucet in the bathtub that doesn't work. I have to carry buckets of water from the kitchen. And there," pointing upward, "are the stains from the roof that has leaked since the day I moved in. That flaking paint – that's not good, is it? And the only way I can watch the television is if I turn off the lights downstairs. Otherwise, everything shuts off."

"Well," I thought to myself, "I feel bad for this woman. But the house and the settlement sheet sure do give me serious evidence." I turned to the homeowner and said, "I'll bet you're pretty angry about the down payment you made."

"I didn't make a down payment."

"Are you sure? Do you have the paperwork from when you bought the house?"

They always did. And, now I had the settlement sheet.

Throughout this ordeal, which gets more and more incredible as we go on, it is the settlement sheet that became the smoking gun. Unfortunately, the settlement sheet is not public information. I knocked on dozens of doors collecting as many as I could.

She hands me the settlement sheet. And, there it is. "It says here that you made a down payment of $6,500."

"I'm telling you, I didn't have any money. I didn't make a down payment."

Homeowner after homeowner, every single one a person of color, many of them with a language barrier, every one of them with an income that didn't support the cost of owning that home, every one having no idea where the information came from on that settlement sheet. I would discover that the perp, meaning the mortgage broker, would take the buyer to the bank in the morning of settlement, deposit the cash, then return after the closing to take the cash back. That's called "fraud."

In every case the lender was an out-of-town, unregulated mortgage finance company that would have no idea that the comparables being used by the appraiser to justify their appraisal weren't legitimate comps. The companies had names like Option One, Ameriquest, New Century and even SLM Financial (yes, sports fans, even Congressionally-chartered Sallie Mae, the company that does student loans, was in the business of ripping off people in the housing market.) With each visit I would get angrier. With each audience I would tell more, naming names, keeping nothing to myself. There was nothing secret about what I was doing. I am far too loose-lipped to keep information like this to myself.

Eventually, I was able to identify more than a dozen co-conspirators. There were the mortgage brokers. There were the appraisers. There were the lenders whose underwriters were either criminally slipshod or lazy or they were co-conspirators (I'm convinced it was the latter). One title insurance company handled all of the settlements – sounds like a co-conspirator. There was one insurance broker who underwrote the homeowners insurance for each of the buyers; sounds like a co-conspirator. There were several investors who bought and flipped the properties. Still more co-conspirators.

Of course, there were special audiences. I sought audiences with my congressman, Pat Toomey, now in the United States Senate, the Bureau of Consumer Protection, which argued that the buyers, because they signed the settlement sheet, were complicit and, therefore, criminals, too. Audiences like the Pennsylvania Department of Banking's top officials, even the man charged with overseeing the licensing of appraisers, one of my best friends, a fraternity brother from Dickinson College, was unable to act. I met with Senate staff. I met with Fannie Mae. I met with state legislators. Nobody gave a shit. I wondered, if these transactions had taken place in different neighborhoods or if the buyers looked more like me or if the value of the homes was greater would the issue have been ignored.

I kept at it. This story worked well as an illustration of what was going on in communities around the country. As a member of the board of directors of the National Community Reinvestment Coalition, the story made for a great illustration in our meetings with top executives of the predatory lenders and still more audiences. Little by little, my homeowners, whose settlement sheets and stories were so valuable, were losing their homes.

I saw the Lehigh County sheriff at a city volleyball league game and told him about what was happening. He acknowledged that the foreclosure rate was rising at a troubling pace. I suggested that he place a moratorium on the foreclosure of any house that had been financed by a subprime lender to determine whether the buyer was a victim of fraud. He seemed interested. So I set a meeting. He invited his solicitor. I made my case. His solicitor responded by saying that the sheriff had no statutory authority to do what I was asking. "But Sheriff, you have the moral authority. What are they going to do? Throw you in jail? You'll be a hero for doing what is right and for protecting people from a massive conspiracy to commit fraud. Hell, I'd go to jail for that." I lost the argument.

A few days later, I got a call from a member of my church who was an attorney in the county solicitor's office. He said, "Alan, do you know who [the solicitor] represents in his private practice? He represents banks." Yes, indeed, the guy conducting the sale of people's foreclosed homes represented the creditors who were taking homes from debtors. Those debtors had no such special representation at the sheriff's office. I felt like I was in some kind of television crime drama.

I was down to about 10 or 12 of my homeowners still in their homes and got word that another would be losing her home to this crazy system of ours. So, on the morning of her sheriff's sale, I showed up with the crew from the local television news station and a reporter from *The Morning Call*. The solicitor says, "Jennings, what are you doing now?" "I said, "The foreclosure on your list was a victim of a conspiracy to commit fraud. I thought that people here in this country cared about the victims. Apparently not, so I'm going to make sure you don't sell that house this morning. You will have to have a deputy or two haul my ass out of here." I figured that would make for some pretty good "film at six," as they say in the television news business. He steps out of the room, returning just a few minutes later, and announces that that sale would be delayed until the end of the proceedings.

That son of a bitch figured the press wouldn't wait. But they did.

The end of the proceedings eventually comes and the solicitor announces that the sale in question would be postponed until the next sale in a month.

Ultimately, I found someone in a position of authority who was interested in the case. Keep in mind, lots of people had already lost their homes. Some of the homes were reacquired and flipped yet again while the clowns we elect and the people we pay as taxpayers twiddled their thumbs. The district attorney felt that we had a case but said it was largely outside his jurisdiction and required much more resources than he could muster. But he did get us an audience with the FBI.

We showed them what we had. The agent present acknowledged that, yes, indeed, this was a crime and well within the jurisdiction of federal prosecutors. "But I have a question. How many victims are there?" I was astonished. The wise guy in me felt like the character in Arlo Guthrie's "Alice's Restaurant;" you know, the guy who was just sitting there on the Group W bench. I grew up watching "The FBI", "Ironside" and countless other law and order programs. The guys in the white hats always showed up, always pursued the case. But here was the FBI apparently having to make a determination of whether this crime was significant enough to justify the deployment of their resources. I was tempted to say, "Sir, we've got nothing but a couple hundred ignorant colored folks who are too damned stupid to understand how we white folks do business." Instead, I handed him my list of more than 200 properties.

I have no idea how many victims would have been acceptable to my government. 30? 100? After all, it's the city, these folks are poor. Plus they have accents. And, they don't look like us.

Apparently, 200 inner-city, low-income people of color made the cut.

I thought we handed the prosecutors a nice, neat case. I figured that all they'd have to do is confirm the information we gave them and "POW!" some sons of bitches would be going to jail. Not so fast: the case took another two years, during which still more people were being ripped off.

Incredibly, the appraisers so critical to the equation, the title company that handled nearly every transaction, the investors who bought and flipped the properties, the homeowners' insurance company that insured the houses – not one was indicted.

More incredibly, those rogues were brought to the sentencing hearing by the defense attorneys, who offered them as character witnesses for the three (that's right, just three) perpetrators who were indicted.

CNN's "Open House," a television newsmagazine that aired on Saturdays, did a segment on mortgage fraud and our case was used as illustration. There I was, on CNN, calling the perps "scum bags."

By now, though, Anthony Mazillo and other heroes of unregulated American commerce had moved on. Maybe they had already ripped off all the dumb poor people in our neighborhoods. Or, in the wild, wild West of Alan Greenspan's libertarian credit system, they had found a new market to exploit, maybe even developed a more imaginative product. It turns out that they had. If what they were doing to poor people was an automatic weapon, the "option ARM" was the nuclear bomb. If the weapon they used on poor people destroyed neighborhood after neighborhood, the nuclear bomb eventually took out the entire international economy.

The so-called option ARM (i.e., "adjustable rate mortgage") was a product used to prey upon the "mine is bigger" market of baby boomers who grew up believing they could have everything. This product would put people in $400,000 houses that should have been buying $250,000 houses. I won't get into the details but here are the basics. Unlike the standard ARM, in which the interest rate ebbs and flows with the market, option ARMs only adjusted upward, the industry assumed all option ARM takers were going to have rapidly rising incomes two years into the purchase, enabling them to either keep up with the adjustment or refinance. Lots didn't. This product was the Hummer of all predatory lending products. And by 2004, some 35 percent of all mortgages were option ARMs.

You see, George Bailey was gone, and, with him, the quaint old days when the same company that booked the loan celebrated with the homeowner when the mortgage was paid off.

In our swashbuckling lead-up to the 2007 collapse, a broker connected the borrower to a lender, too often an unregulated mortgage finance company. An originator booked the loan. The lender sold the mortgage on the secondary market. Massive tranches of loans in the hundreds of billions of dollars were assembled, insured by big companies like AIG. Incredibly, none of these players along the way held the mortgage long enough to be responsible for its performance until a tranche loaded with bad loans collapsed. Remember, in the lead up to 2007, some 35 percent of all mortgages were these predatory option ARMs that were almost designed to fail.

Then there were "stated income" loans. We called them "liar loans." The borrower wouldn't have to prove any of their claims made to get a loan.

We'd learned this lesson before.

Here we were, squawking to anyone who would listen, shouting that the sky was falling. Except that, in this case, it really was. And it did. All along the way, activists like me, led by the National Community Reinvestment Coalition, were begging lawmakers and regulators to stop the shenanigans. People in key places were informed about and later warned about the impending disaster.

So there I was, this guy from Allentown, Pennsylvania, who had worked his ass off trying to push the system around, getting it to improve access to credit for regular folks, standing in awe in the Board of Governors conference room at the Federal Reserve, begging the chairman to stop the bull shit. And what does the chairman do? He invokes Ayn Rand, for God's sake. "I'm a libertarian when it comes to access to credit," says, arguably, the second most powerful man in the world. "Why would someone take out a loan on such abusive terms in the first place?"

When the shit hit the fan, Atlas shrugged, "who knew?" I couldn't believe one of the most venerable and respected men in the world (up until that point, that is) publicly claimed he had no idea a cauldron was bubbling, about to blow. I publicly called him a liar. I had personal knowledge, having been in the room when we presented him the facts, all of us – activists that had fought this battle from every angle we could find or create – knew it was inevitable that the shit would, indeed, hit the fan.

This country has a knack for defying its own claims to moral righteousness. It was a financial bacchanalia, but only a few were invited. They were ignoring lessons that had been learned before, a handful of people making mountains of money, most of whom should've gone to jail. Meanwhile, Americans – innocent people, workaday people playing by the rules, believing in the system, saluting the flag - were being screwed. They were losing their homes, their property values were tanking; what little wealth they had scraped together was being stripped. It was enough to make me sick. We tried everything. We used every tool in the toolbox.

As Bruce Springsteen sang, in "Jack of All Trades," "A banker man grows fat, working man grows thin, it all happened before, it will happen again."

There they were, those lying bastards who defended and even protected the perpetrators, trying to revise history by claiming it was the fault of the community reinvestment activists because we had pushed banks to do loans they shouldn't have been doing. It was my fault. One of the most vocal politicians pushing the lie was my own former congressman who was now running for the U.S. Senate.

So, there are some basic facts: First, every bank regulator appointed by then-President George W. Bush publicly and clearly made statements rejecting the claim being made by liars like Pat Toomey.

The Community Reinvestment Act does not require banks to make bad loans; in fact, everyone in the industry knows that protection of safety and soundness always trumps any pro-consumer measures. And anyway, would someone like me want people who have mountains of money make much more by ripping off struggling Americans? After years of trying to help neighborhoods recover, would we want them to go back and strip the neighborhood of whatever wealth it's tried to retain if not create? Also, the law applies only to regulated banks. But it wasn't the banks – at least not the more local and regional banks – that were doing the irresponsible lending; it was the unregulated mortgage finance companies like Countrywide, Ameriquest, New Century and SLM Financial.

In our homeownership counseling seminars our message on sub-prime mortgages was that if you needed one, that was God's way of telling you that you weren't ready to buy a house; stop, save some money, improve your credit score and buy a house you can afford.

Pat Toomey has to know better. If not, his Harvard MBA isn't worth the paper on which it is printed. And, yet, he pushed The Great Lie on the American people.

And people wonder why I'm so damned angry.

What do I do about this, one of the most irresponsible, outrageous, sinister examples of unmitigated greed and its hired guns? If I go on the offensive and point out that the senator was being dishonest, I run the risk of losing key supporters who love Pat Toomey. Also, going on the offensive will look like it's motivated by partisanship, a no-no in our field. And it violates one of my suggestions earlier in this book: Try really hard not to burn bridges. Well, here's the thing: Ideologues like Senator Toomey can't restrain themselves. They will never compromise. They will always side with crippling government to prove it doesn't work by ensuring it can't work.

Sometimes you have to burn the damn bridge.

Chapter 24

Lest You Think It's Been All Successes and No Failures…

WE'VE FAILED PLENTY. HERE ARE SOME OF THE BIGGER ONES.

SHARED-USE COMMERCIAL KITCHEN
A shared-use commercial kitchen is an incubator for food-related businesses. We got the idea from a pretty cool project in Poughkeepsie, New York, one of many small Northeast cities that have lost a lot of population and a ton of tax base. The concept is a fully-equipped incubator for food businesses to become the next Famous Amos cookies. We put together a solid business plan, having interviewed dozens of prospective users of the kitchen to determine what kind of equipment they would need, how often they would want to use it and how much rent they could afford to pay. We ran into all kinds of obstacles, such as a developer who had a building that was not exactly what we wanted but the only one that came close to what we needed. When we offered him the price at which he had the property listed the SOB raised the price. Another owner of a building that would have been perfect refused to give us one month to get a zoning variance on the use of the property, preferring to accept the offer made by a company that bought blood from addicts and other desperate people.

We were able to work around these obstacles and had raised more than $2 million for the project but never anticipated the hijacking of four planes that became weapons in a despicable, ages-old biblical conflict when they were flown into three high-profile buildings and one into the ground. Everything stopped at that point: Philanthropists stopped giving and then-Governor Tom Ridge (Pennsylvania) called in and canceled contracts.

NEW NEIGHBORHOOD CREDIT UNION

We wanted to create a "poor people's bank." We had more than $1 million in capital pledged from several banks as well as more than $100,000 per year in operating subsidies. However, the National Credit Union Administration would not approve a community development charter for a community credit union with a "field of membership" that was not in contiguous communities. Not long after we gave up, the NCUA reversed itself and began approving such projects. By then we and the banks that had committed to us had moved on.

NEW MARKETS TAX CREDITS

Twice we spent tens of thousands of dollars on consultants attempting to get New Markets Tax Credits to strengthen the resurgent redevelopment of Allentown's downtown. Thanks to one of the most aggressive tools available to any city in America, nearly $1 billion in new development is revitalizing Pennsylvania's third largest city. Our proposal would have provided the resources to ensure the "rising tide lifted all boats," by extending a variety of opportunities into the distressed neighborhoods surrounding the downtown.

Anyone who has ever come in contact with New Markets Tax Credits knows that this extraordinarily complex development tool is a full employment program for consultants who have very specialized but obscure financial skills. This program is, simply, a classic example of why so many Americans hate their government. Nevertheless, we tried twice and failed twice.

We had failures, all right. Hopefully, we've learned from each one.

Chapter 25

"He's Only Happy When He's Fighting Mad"

THAT WAS THE TITLE OF A FEATURE ARTICLE ABOUT ME IN A LOCAL MAGAZINE CALLED LEHIGH VALLEY MAGAZINE BACK IN 2002. Nice article. Accurate title.

About the time I was being diagnosed with a chronic, progressive neuromuscular disease the doctor told me he thought I was depressed. I rolled my eyes. It wasn't the first time a guy with a medical degree made that claim.

"I'm not depressed."

"I want you to go see a counselor," he said.

"I've been to counseling. It doesn't work. I'm smarter than they are."

"I'm going to send you to one you can't manipulate."

I rolled my eyes again. I didn't want to be a typical guy who won't get medical attention for the health problems he might have. So, I went to see the counselor to whom I was referred.

After some obligatory small talk, he told me to tell him why I thought I was sent to him.

"The world is totally fucked up. You know that; I know that. Depressed people can't get off the couch. I jump out of bed every morning, race to work and fight like hell on behalf of people who need me. I come home at night, sleep as little as necessary (sleep is a waste of time), jump out of bed the next morning, race to work and fight like hell on behalf of people who need me. I'm not depressed. I'm pissed. What's the problem with that?"

The doctor (who, by the way, didn't accept third-party insurance payments, totally pissing me off) said I had some kind of issue that a friend who is a psychologist said doesn't exist, said there was nothing he could do about it, that the world is a better place because of me, and told me I could go.

"Another one bites the dust," I thought. The Queen song was stuck in my head for the rest of the day.

Chapter 26

Got a World View? Get One!

"If you don't stand for something, you'll fall for anything."
—Hell if I know who said this!

"If you don't know where you're going, how are you supposed to get there and how will you know when you did?"
—I don't know this one, either

BUT THEY SURE MAKE SENSE, DON'T THEY? Like clarifying your values to ensure you know why you want to save the world, standing for something matters. Understand your world.

I know what's wrong. I think I know how to make it right. Whole volumes have been written on this stuff. But I'm not writing a 1,200-page tome. I want folks to actually read this. So, here is what's wrong with the world … OK, here's what's wrong in many of our communities.

PROVING GOVERNMENT DOESN'T WORK BY ENSURING IT CAN'T WORK
We might have the world's largest economy but we also have one of the most lopsided. Too few have too much. Our democracy cannot function without a middle class. I think there is a direct connection between the diminishing middle class and the decline in participation in civic life. People think the system is rigged. And it is. The notorious Koch brothers do not care if people participate; they only care about getting as much as they can – enough wealth, enough stuff, enough power. They are blocking regular folks from participation by funding these idiotic "voter ID"

schemes, buying a Supreme Court that had the audacity to find that our democracy can somehow thrive when corporations are considered people and extended the same rights. That argument might be even more ludicrous than the decision to hand George W. Bush the presidency in 2000. They don't believe in government, they hate paying taxes, they don't think we have any need for rules that require our safety and health to be protected or that everyone be able to pay their bills. They relentlessly attack government, claiming it doesn't work. They succeed at cutting programs. When those programs fail because they were so underfunded, they gawk and point out how ineffective government is. They make sure that government doesn't work by choking it of its ability to work. See? It doesn't work. They're brilliant, and we're letting them get away with it.

If the rules are stacked, then why bother participating? Why join the PTA? Why donate to charity?

TOO FEW OF THEM, TOO MANY OF US
I'm not citing the data. We all know it. The economy is working just fine for the lucky few. They are accumulating larger and larger shares of the income and even greater shares of the wealth.

OUR "WELFARE" SYSTEM SUCKS
That word, the "w" word, has been hijacked. It played a pretty prominent role in our nation's founding, right there in the Preamble to one of the most venerable documents in history – our history:

"We the people of the United States, in Order to form a more perfect Union, establish Justice, insure domestic Tranquility, provide for the common defence, promote the general Welfare, and secure the Blessings of Liberty to ourselves and our Posterity, do ordain and establish this Constitution for the United States of America."

Those commies, the old white men who wrote the Constitution, thought it a pretty good word.

Today, however, Americans have grown to hate it. It has become synonymous with "sloth," carries bigoted undertones and is used by the Right to describe every program designed to make poverty less painful in an attempt to undermine any suggestion that government has any responsibility for those our economy fails.

I hate our welfare system. If it is intended to provide any semblance of a minimum standard of living for the least of those among us, it is a complete failure. The federal government pays 55 percent of the tab, the states pay the rest. But the states set the amount people will receive (within certain constraints).

When I am speaking to groups here, I often challenge them with a barrage of questions.

- How much does a Pennsylvania family of three with no other income collect monthly in "welfare" (what we now call "Temporary Assistance for Needy Families")?

    The answers I get from good people who are incredibly ignorant always exceed $800, with some as high as $2,000.

    Fact: That mom and her two children will receive $403 per month.

- When was the last time Pennsylvania increased that amount?

    Silence.

    Fact: Pennsylvania last raised its allowance from $384 in January, 1985.

- Out of roughly 630,000 people in the Lehigh Valley, how many are collecting TANF?

    The answers vary widely, amazingly, some as high as 30 percent.

    Fact: Barely 6,000 people (not households, but people), or .9 percent. And this data is from the mid- to late-1980s, in the middle of one of the worst recoveries in American history.

- What is the average size of a family receiving TANF in Pennsylvania?

    The answers by now no longer shock me: 4? 5? 7?

    Fact: The average family on welfare is comprised of 2.1 people, not 2.1 kids, but a total, including the parent(s), of 2.1.

So, why do we spend so much energy condemning and trying to kill this most basic of family safety nets?

OUR SOCIETY IS FAR MORE THREATENED WHEN POVERTY AND DESPAIR LEAD TO DEPENDENCE AND APATHY THAN WHEN IT LEADS TO ANGER AND ACTIVISM

I said that already. OK, so it bears repeating.

WHY DO WE SUBSIDIZE RICH FOLKS' BEACH HOUSES WHILE SO MANY OTHERS ARE HOMELESS?
In 2013, this nation spent $101 billion on the mortgage interest deduction, commonly considered a sacred cow among the middle class. The idea is that this tax subsidy will help enable more folks to own their own home, something so sacrosanct that we call it The American Dream. Gosh, that sounds nice doesn't it? It does, though, sound a bit like, "If you don't own your own home, you ain't no American."

Did you catch that? One hundred one billion dollars. That looks like this: $101,000,000,000.

Here's the thing: 77 percent of that mortgage interest deduction subsidy went to households with incomes in excess of $100,000. What really riles me is that a family with a $700,000 mortgage is eligible for the subsidy. What really, really riles me is that we generous taxpayers will even subsidize a family's vacation home at the beach.

That might be OK if other needs are being met. But last year, in our little corner of Pennsylvania, we provided shelter for 2,500 homeless people. Say what? You heard me, there are hundreds of thousands of homeless people in our country and we have determined that families with enough money to have a second house at the beach are more important than a homeless child and her family having any home at all.

OUR PUBLIC EDUCATION SYSTEM IS THE MOST EFFECTIVE WAY WE LOCK INEQUITY INTO OUR SOCIETY.
If you're being honest with yourself, you must already know this.

But don't interpret that to mean that I support privatizing or "charterizing" our schools. Quite the opposite. Public education should be the great leveler of the playing field. By using the property tax as the primary vehicle for funding public education, it ensures that those who've got the most have the entire ladder between them and those poor folks at the bottom, who can't even reach the damned thing, much less pull themselves up.

BEHAVIORAL HEALTH PROBLEMS (MENTAL ILLNESS AND DRUG AND/OR ALCOHOL ADDICTION) ARE TEARING US APART.
The hospitals know this; it is that apparent. Many are sitting on hundreds of millions of dollars of their community's money, knowing that the need is at tragic levels.

The good news is that the Affordable Care Act is forcing the reimbursement system to pay for outcomes, not just procedures. So, if a hospital does a procedure, then sends the patient home and he proceeds to return to his opioid addiction, that procedure has the proverbial snowball's chance of being successful. Don't look now, but hospitals – at least the ones run by smart people – are starting to figure this out. This actually has the potential to bring some good news to the equation.

IF YOU HAVE A RACIST FRIEND, NOW IS THE TIME FOR YOUR FRIENDSHIP TO END.
I shouldn't need to say any more about this one.

But I probably should tell you, to avoid getting nabbed by the plagiarism Nazis, that the subtitle, above, is the name of a song by a defunct British band called Special AKA.

THE MARKET DOESN'T WORK FOR THE LABOR SUPPLY ANYMORE
Wage stagnation might be the most challenging issue of our time. We simply aren't seeing wage growth even as the economy continues to grow and jobs are being created. It defies the rule of economics.

Unions used to be the way regular folks could gain enough power to actually intervene in the prevailing forces of the economy. Unfortunately, they've been decimated.

Then there's the minimum wage. It needs to go up. I would argue $10.10 an hour was outdated not long after it was announced as the legislative goal in 2013. How about $15 per hour in 2020? I risk dating this book with these suggestions but the point really is that we must insist on the wage going up every two years by the amount of inflation since the prior increase. It will always lag, but at least we won't have to fight this battle over and over while the purchasing power of the wage continues to decline.

And the longer the working class puts up with it, the wider the gap will be, because you can guarantee the privileged folks are getting the best advice. So their piece of the pie is getting pretty self-indulgent. Meanwhile, regular folks are getting smaller and smaller crumbs.

This all, then, reinforces itself. The quality of a public education today depends largely on where you live. Where you live also determines who you know. Who you know determines where you work. Where you work will determine where you live … get the picture?

MEMO TO THE MIDDLE CLASS: WHICH SIDE ARE YOU ON?
You have to give Frank Luntz, the Republicans' top wordsmith, and the spinmeisters on the right credit. They are far outnumbered. Yet they are geniuses with the language. They understand which words work and which ones don't.

They have this uncanny ability to stay on message. And they have no qualms about playing games with the facts (that means they're good liars). In fact, they will repeat the lie over and over until it becomes the truth.

Ronald Reagan was great at this stuff. He developed a missile, technically named the MX, that violated all the non-proliferation agreements. They called it "The Peace Keeper." Impressive.

Then there is the "Clear Skies Initiative." Who's against clear skies? That initiative was, but who's watching?

How about "clean coal?" Even Barack Obama got sucked into that one.

The left? We're too honest. Take Obama's signature campaign agenda: expanding health care to the nearly 50 million Americans left out. The key piece of that legislation was a hybrid between Richard Nixon (that commie), Newt Gingrich (another lefty, eh?) and the Mitt Romney who was governor of Massachusetts. We called it "The Public Option." Hell, why didn't we just call it "The Government Boondoggle?!" It got trashed.

So, here these guys are, largely from the fringe of the party with a bunch of rednecks, a few rich guys and a ton of intolerant people, convincing regular Americans that guns, gay marriage and abortion are more important than their kids' education, clean air and water and the minimum wage. Damn, they're good. And, boy, are we getting our asses kicked.

What really annoys me … OK, "annoys" isn't the right word. What totally pisses me off is that middle class Americans align themselves with the rich more than they do the poor.

Part of the reason for this is that the right has been so effective at turning people on welfare into lazy bums who don't want to work. Do you want to pay taxes on your hard-earned income to support some lazy bum with a nice car and the latest, fancy entertainment system?

Can anyone really say, with a straight face, given the enormous disparities in income and assets in America, that someone in the middle class has anything but the slightest possibility of rising into the ranks of the wealthy rather than falling into the ranks of the poor? We all know someone, I'm sure, who pulled off the old Horatio Alger trick. I know several. But I know plenty times more who have been left behind.

People want desperately to believe that the promise of America that we all were taught in seventh grade social studies remains a promise. I hate to break it to you, folks, but most of us aren't that lucky.

One of the policy think tanks should do the research and examine the disparity in likelihood that someone in the middle class is going to climb up rather than fall back. We could turn that ratio (my guess is that it's probably in the range of 50 or more to one) into a simple organizing and outreach campaign along the lines of the old "69 cents" campaign pointing out how women earn so much less than men. Billboards, bumper stickers, tweets, t-shirts with the simple message:

50:1
You haven't got a chance.

That ought to do it. We could get Bruce Springsteen to write a song:

> Fifty to one
> You haven't got a chance
> They want us to believe
> But there won't be no dance.

I wonder what Frank Luntz would come up with to counter that.

SACRIFICE
We need to make this part of our lives. We can do better by others.

It is very common when I speak to an audience that I am asked what people can do to help. They are expecting me to suggest, among other things, donating money, I'm sure. And I do. But I throw them a curve. I point out that the most people typically give is, maybe, 10 percent of their income. That is admirable. But they can do so much more by thinking about how best to spend the 90 percent or more they keep for themselves. They can start by embracing the concept of doing no harm. But if they take the concept seriously enough, they can do some good by how they spend their disposable income.

If you're concerned about suburban sprawl, then don't buy a house on a half-acre lot on a cul-de-sac; buy a more modest home, preferably in a town or city. Density is the best way to preserve open space.

If you're concerned about the behavior of big, publicly-traded corporations, buy their stock and become an activist shareholder, demanding better environmental stewardship, better treatment of their workers, fewer sprints to foreign lands to exploit cheap labor.

Don't enrich the big-box companies that take their profits home with them. Instead, go out of your way to patronize locally-owned businesses. Make a special effort to support businesses in depressed communities, especially those owned by people of color.

When I spend money I try to consider how my decisions will affect the market and, by extension, communities, income and wealth disparities, and the environment. The better the market, the fairer it can be, the less money is needed to sustain surplus labor (meaning those left out of the job market), and the more equitable the tax base can be.

Chapter 27

Jenningsisms: The Words We Choose

THE MESSAGE MATTERS. So does getting that message across. If you have ever attended more than one rally for a single presidential candidate you know that the candidate has a "stump speech." That stump speech is why so much reporting is about the "horse race," rather than the issues during a presidential campaign. That speech is used over and over and cynical reporters get sick of it quickly. Their minds and their attention wander off and, before you know it, the news story has little to do with the substance of the campaign. The candidates, on the other hand, know that they must say the same thing, over and over, pounding it into our thick heads to make sure we are getting the message.

I have made at least 300 speeches over the course of my 35-year career. There were surely more than 8,000 people in those audiences. I don't think I have made the same speech twice but I certainly use some of the same phrases over and over again. I have developed the message over time and am convinced that I am making the point as creatively, as effectively and, hopefully, as memorably as I can. I call them "Jenningsisms" for lack of a better and more modest term. I guess I could call them "My Stupid Sayings."

Here they are, some of which I used in making previous points just a few pages ago:

- How can we expect people to think about their long-term career goals when they are not sure where their next meal is coming from?
- The highest form of self-sufficiency is citizenship.

- We don't do anything for anyone.
- CACLV is an agency with an attitude.
- Charity is something you do when you don't have justice. We pursue justice.
- When our society turns its back on its children it should not be surprised when those children grow up to turn their backs on society.
- Our society is far more threatened when poverty leads to apathy and dependence than when it leads to anger and activism.
- Patience is not a virtue; it is the luxury of the affluent, the powerful, the comfortable. Don't ask me to be patient on behalf of folks who are none of those.
- The best community development program is called a "profit."
- The old anti-poverty strategy of helping people get out of the 'hood was a mistake. If we help the winners escape and leave the losers behind, we concede the permanent ghetto. I'd rather strengthen our neighborhoods so the winners want to stay and there are no losers.
- Anger is simply passion with an edge.
- I am cynical enough to know what I'm up against but optimistic enough to pick the fight anyway.
- Our ideology is only as useful as its practical application.
- You can't have a functioning community without a functioning marketplace, and you can't have a functioning marketplace if everyone is poor.
- If you believe in a free market, you have to believe in it being a fair market.
- How we govern and fund public education has become our most effective means for locking inequity into our society.
- I think of myself as being cynical enough to know what I'm up against, but optimistic enough to pick the fight, anyway.
- You can't really help someone who doesn't want to help him/herself.

Chapter 28

The Words We Choose, Part 2

NICE PEOPLE, PEOPLE WHO THINK WE SHOULD BE MORE INCLUSIVE, PEOPLE WHO UNDERSTAND THAT WE CAN HURT PEOPLE WITH THE WORDS WE CHOOSE, YOU KNOW, LIKE SECOND GRADE TEACHERS AND MR. ROGERS, SUGGEST WE COULD BE A LITTLE MORE FRIENDLY, A LITTLE MORE SENSITIVE IF WE WERE MORE CAREFUL WITH OUR LANGUAGE. Sounds like a nice thought to me, one that would indicate that our civility has evolved.

We can't have that, say the people who apparently don't like the idea of being more thoughtful toward others. Believe it or not, they turn this concept into a bad thing, labeling it "political correctness." No, it's just being more civil, more thoughtful. Doesn't matter, say they, we like the old, nasty, who-cares-how-you-feel approach. We like having our jackboots on your throat.

I suppose, like anything else, we can take the concept a bit too far. For example, what is the politically correct term for a white male? Oppressor. That's a good one! They mock people for trying to find a better way to bring us all together. That's because a divided society works well for some of those among us.

Having said all of that, we do need to find common ground on the language. If we come off sounding like we eat too much granola or whatever the foodies are touting these days, we allow ourselves to become caricatures, we look and sound like pointy-headed liberals or condescending elitists.

This country needs to have a productive, constructive discussion on race. In my judgment, there has been little real progress on race issues in my lifetime. My conservative friends forcefully argue otherwise. They are sick of the issue of race. Their attitude goes something like this: "Why are you sticking this in my face? I don't own any slaves!"

They don't get it. To be sure, the water fountains no longer say, "Whites Only." But we still have "whites only" cul-de-sacs, "whites only" country clubs and even "whites only" boards of directors overseeing many non-profits. Our schools are particularly segregated and scores on standardized tests reflect that. And, yet, those who have been losing the most due to discrimination and those with the most to gain as a result of its abolition are not allowed to talk about it. That seems to be the very definition of oppression.

What I find in attempting to stimulate discussion on race is that our hypersensitivity to words stifles debate. Consequently, people of color are not getting the information they need to participate in the debate and they aren't really hearing whites when they speak in the coded language they've been forced to adopt because of how embarrassing it is when someone calls them on their politically incorrect choice of words. I'm not suggesting that people of color should be forced to hear that ugly word no one is allowed to say but a productive discussion requires hearing as well as speaking. When someone ignorantly uses the wrong word we should see it as a teaching opportunity, not an opportunity to excoriate.

SO, HERE ARE SOME OF THE WORDS THAT WORK AND SOME THAT DON'T
These work: *opportunity, fairness, neighbor, service, stewardship, promise, respect, earn, sacrifice, private, us*

These don't: *client, entitlement, equality, guarantee, urban, collect, public, welfare, them*

Chapter 29

Advice for the Activist Without Institutional Ramparts

OK, SO YOU DON'T WANT TO COMMIT YOUR WHOLE LIFE TO THE FIGHT; MAYBE YOU HAVE THE IDEA THAT YOU SHOULD HAVE A LITTLE MORE BALANCE BETWEEN OBSESSIVE-COMPULSIVE WORKAHOLISM AND ENJOYING LIFE BLISSFULLY IGNORANT. Maybe you just want to do good volunteer work and can't afford to give it all up for the cause. I'm cool with that.

So, here is a collection of advice born from almost 40 years of wins and losses and the lessons that come from both of them.

- **First,** try as hard as you can to find a way to avoid creating a new nonprofit. There are already too many (they spend too much time trying to sustain themselves, struggle to be entrepreneurial, they often duplicate existing effort);
- **Second,** much of what you are reading in this book applies;
- **Third,** make sure you know the right people who know the right people, if you know what I mean;
- **Fourth,** in any organizing effort, it's important that you hit lots of singles, but …
- **Fifth,** Earl Weaver, the colorful, late Hall of Fame manager of the Baltimore Orioles, would tell you how valuable a three-run home run is (in other words, get some heavy hitters).

Photograph courtesy of Keenan-Nagle Advertising, Inc.

Section IV

In My Life

Chapter 30

"The Rap on You is You're Manipulative"

A LONG-TERM BOARD MEMBER SAID THAT TO ME.

Pause.

"Well, that's a good thing, right?"

Anyway, "manipulative" is a strong word. I prefer to say that I try to persuade people to do things they wouldn't do if I didn't bug them. I feel like that's all I ever do.

Then there's this one, closely related:

"The ends justify the means." Niccolo Machiavelli gets the credit (or the blame) for that one, although the phrase is nowhere to be found in the pages of his 16th century book, "The Prince." So, the source of the quote is up for grabs. I'm tempted to claim it. More than once I've suggested that some of the things I have done would make Machiavelli blush. But the relativist in me finds it hard to embrace the full range of possible means and the ends are not always important enough to use any mean to achieve them.

Understand, I would go a long way down paths most would never even enter. Yes, I would break the law. Yes, I would use secrets.

But the most powerful tool available to serious change agents is "reputational risk." It requires you to fully understand the rules of engaging the news media.

This conversation has the potential to get me in trouble. But, hell, I've been using these tools of my trade for decades and it's worked pretty well.

REALLY, THIS IS ALL ABOUT RELATIONSHIPS

I don't mean that I am manipulating people, especially not the many in my community who I appreciate, trust, respect, even love. But I do use relationships to advance the cause. I know I may well be the most hated person in the Lehigh Valley. But I work hard at most relationships to at least avoid that "hated" category.

I am proud of the relationships I have established. Some of my best friends are people with whom I almost completely disagree. In my 35 years of fighting these battles I may be proudest of the extent to which people who most embrace and benefit from the status quo are my friends. Many are not just friends but significant supporters of the work we do.

Chapter 31

"The Only Thing in the Middle of the Road in This Country are Armadillos and Yellow Stripes"

—Jim Hightower

THAT'S A GREAT QUOTE. Jim Hightower is a plainspoken, straight-shooting progressive from Texas, of all places, who was the Commissioner of Agriculture and sometime radio personality. The problem is that he's wrong. I think something like 60 percent of the American people are moderates. About 20 percent are kooky, well-armed, white reactionaries who aren't smart enough or have a big enough heart to open their eyes and consider a different point of view. Another 20 percent on the other end of the extremes are folks who are at least as dug in, look down their noses at those who aren't, in their minds, smart enough to be enlightened and who have no common sense about what it takes to solve our problems.

When it comes right down to it, our ideology is useless without its practical application.

Like it or not, we have a market economy. It produces big winners; it produces lots of losers. Lots. And lots.

There is much to be said for competition: it motivates people to win by excelling. If everybody is doing their best the expected outcome is, well, doing their best. In my mind, we all benefit. If, somehow, a loss is too great then we have to, as a matter of civility and on behalf of community, show some humanity and rally the community. We should also do what we can to intervene in the market to minimize the damage that can be done by that market. Theoretically, the bigger the pie the bigger each piece we get.

So, the role my agency has chosen is to insert ourselves into the equation. We think we are pretty good at projecting how the various forces in our culture, economy and political system will play themselves out.

My conservative friends like to think that everyone can make a go of it. If they didn't, they'd have to concede that it is the market and its very nature, not the "losers," that is flawed. My lefty friends think we can tax the shit out of the wealthy and they will stay in whatever jurisdiction it is that raises their taxes. The problem is that there are countless ways to avoid paying your fair share and whole industries (ever hear of Wall Street?) that exist for the purpose of showing them how. And there are countries eagerly awaiting rich Americans' wealth to hide in their banks.

So, now, what do we do about all of that? I suppose we can continue to live in a house or, more accurately, nation divided. We already know where that will take us. Have you seen the news lately? Innocent people, whether they are studying the Bible or attending elementary school or having an office party, are being slaughtered. Heroin addiction is approaching epidemic levels again. People are scared to travel for fear of being beheaded. Our health care system still sucks. And we have so poisoned the environment that we are threatening the species itself. I fear for my kids and am petrified for my grandchildren.

IT STARTS WITH SACRIFICE
We used to use that word. It's one of those words that means so much but got lost. Maybe because we don't believe in it. Maybe because the folks who hate just about everyone, especially poor people, are bitterly opposed to doing anything like the things they go to church every Sunday to hear and be lectured about that Jesus of Nazareth did.

Those of you on the left who are all smug in your insistence you're right about rich people and that government is bought and sold to promote the agendas of the lucky few should recognize that we aren't very good at government. And just because you have an ideological adherence to the notion that the government should be the Great Protector doesn't mean that you are off the hook with respect to making your own charitable donations.

Then there is the question of how, exactly, we address the needs of those not lucky enough to be blessed with marketable skills or whose skills are just not worth much in the increasingly complex and fast-changing demands of the modern marketplace. It seems to me that we only have a few choices: We can do nothing as those families deteriorate into depravity, then take their kids and put the men in jail; we can invest in them and hope that the investment pays off; or we can give them a civilized amount of support (I can't use the term "welfare"). Only the first of those options should be ruled out. Ironically (I hate irony), that's the one our nation has basically chosen by default.

When I was in college the idea of saving the world meant focusing my attention on international issues. It didn't take me long to realize, though, that the most powerful country in the world has a fair amount of culpability for some of the more troublesome developments in our world and that, perhaps, my attention should be focused on getting this country's priorities right. However, having started my career just a few weeks after the election of Ronald Reagan, I eventually realized that too few wanted the federal government to have anything to do with social and/or economic justice.

Well, given the role state government has in setting welfare payments, community planning and education, maybe I should focus on getting state government going in the right direction. Hah! Pennsylvania politics is fundamentally corrupt, with only a few elected positions having any power whatsoever; those few almost always place their loyalty to their party caucuses ahead of what's best for their constituents and their neighborhoods. Alas, that leaves local government. Yikes. OK, that leaves private action. It gets rather depressing, doesn't it?

Chapter 32

And Here's Where I Am

ALMOST 400 YEARS AGO, JOHN DONNE SHOWED THE WORLD HOW A CIVILIZED SOCIETY BEHAVES

No man is an island, entire of itself.
Every man is a piece of the continent, a part of the main…
Any man's death diminishes me,
Because I am involved in mankind,
And therefore never send to know for whom the bell tolls;
It tolls for thee.

John Donne
1624

AND HERE IS HOW I MIGHT PUT IT, IN THE TWENTY-FIRST CENTURY

You say you did it.
I say you didn't.
You say you worked hard.
I say, so did I.

You say you worked hard.
I say, so did I.
I say you got lucky.
You say, I didn't try.

> *So, you say it all worked.*
> *I say, not for me.*
> *You say I didn't try.*
> *I say, you just don't see why.*
>
> *You say I didn't try.*
> *I ask, can't you cry?*
> *You ask, why should I?*
> *I ask as I sigh:*
>
> *Why can't you see it?*
> *If we exist as I,*
> *Too few will make it*
> *If we*
> *Are only I.*

Friends, we really are all in this together. A few of us might be able to empty our bank accounts and safe-deposit boxes and flee for some country that is happy to launder our funds. A few others might be able to hole themselves up in some 6' x 8' house made from a kit a la Ted Kaczynski, also known as "The Unabomber" (Google him), load it up with weapons, and hide. But the rest of us need each other. In today's world, almost all of us are dependent on someone else in some form – they grow our food, they refine crude oil into gasoline, they inform or educate us, they buy our products, they protect our safety, they wait on our tables, they save our lives. The point is that "self-sufficient" sounds like a synonym for anti-social. It would be nice if everybody could be financially self-sufficient. But even that would require debate to determine what that means, considering that every one of us who has a mortgage to finance our home and uses the mortgage interest deduction is getting a government subsidy. And that is just one example.

CREATING NEIGHBORHOODS THAT PEOPLE DON'T WANT TO FLEE
So, let's not do anti-poverty work or community development in a way that constantly drains our oldest, most challenged neighborhoods of their best talent and resources. Let's, instead, make those neighborhoods a place where

the winners choose not to leave and one where there are no losers. That means changing the agenda in such a fundamental way that we first think about our neighborhood or community, what it needs and how we can help. How can we grow the tax base? How can we make our streets safer? Where do we get the resources to make our schools educate better? How do we make our market more functional? Where do we find the resources to light up our neighborhood and rob the creeps of their hiding places? How about decorative streetlights, murals and parks? How do we replace the sidewalks, plant more trees, install crosswalks, create bike lanes?

BUILDING ASSETS, CREATING WEALTH, STABILIZING NEIGHBORHOODS
There is a consensus around the idea that homeownership stabilizes neighborhoods. That is not to say that rentals destabilize neighborhoods but when someone owns something they protect it. Nobody washes a rental car. People who own their own homes are more likely to be active citizens, calling the cops, joining the PTA, keeping an eye out for the neighbors' kids, voting. Being a homeowner, especially in a stable or, even better, vibrant neighborhood builds wealth.

What if every one of us made decisions that first considered the impact of that decision on others, our community, our country, the environment? What if we put ourselves last in the pecking order? I would posit that our world would be a much better place for many, many more people and, likely, even ourselves.

Chapter 33

Did You Get the Main Points?

EVERYONE WHO HAS BEEN KIND ENOUGH TO CRITIQUE THE DRAFT OF THIS BOOK HAS TOLD ME THAT I NEED TO MAKE IT CLEAR WHAT THE HANDFUL OF KEY TAKE-HOME POINTS ARE. I have been tempted to resist. I am not going to spoon-feed this stuff. If you're not serious enough to have read this book because you are passionate about making a difference, I'm not going to cooperate.

But, then again, this world needs a lot more change agents. And that's what this book is all about. It would be tempting to put a pop quiz in right here, but few would participate in the exercise, so let's skip past that and just present them, straight up:

WHACK UPSIDE THE HEAD #1
If you're getting into the world of change agent, put everything you've got into it; otherwise, do it as a hobby or as a volunteer.

WHACK UPSIDE THE HEAD #2
Get an attitude and learn how to use it.

WHACK UPSIDE THE HEAD #3
Charity is what society does when it doesn't have justice. Pursue justice.

WHACK UPSIDE THE HEAD #4
Don't do anything for anyone.

WHACK UPSIDE THE HEAD #5
Get your board of directors right.

WHACK UPSIDE THE HEAD #6
Learn how and prepare to use "reputational risk" as a tool.

WHACK UPSIDE THE HEAD #7
Stay clean.

WHACK UPSIDE THE HEAD #8
Get an obsession for responsible stewardship.

WHACK UPSIDE THE HEAD #9
Raising hell and raising money go hand in hand.

WHACK UPSIDE THE HEAD #10
Learn how to use power and don't be shy about it.

WHACK UPSIDE THE HEAD #11
Our ideology is only as useful as its practical application.

But let's sum it all up. With each new day, more and more of us have grown up in a world that almost forces attention deficit disorder on us: Sesame Street, then MTV, on to the Internet, text messages and Twitter. So, if you read just one paragraph in this entire screed, it should be this one:

Our world, our nation, our state, our community, our neighborhood, our lives can be better. If you want to be driving the bus that takes us there, etch these three things into your psyche: if you are not fully committed to the sacrificial and zealous pursuit of the cause, find a different field; be prepared to throw the high, inside fastball; obsess over responsible stewardship and governance in all you do.

I hope the other 204 pages weren't too boring.

Chapter 34

Don't Give Up

THIS IS WHERE WE IDEALISTS, WE INSURGENTS, WE BELIEVERS, WE CHANGE AGENTS (BY NOW, THIS DEEP INTO THIS BOOK, I HOPE THAT INCLUDES YOU) DIG IN, STAND UP, SPEAK OUT, FISTS CLENCHED, TEETH GRITTED AND REJECT CYNICISM, FATALISM, AND FOLLOW THE GUIDANCE OF, ARGUABLY, THE MOST RESPECTED CONSERVATIVE OF THE 20TH CENTURY, WINSTON CHURCHILL.

In a speech to his alma mater, Churchill famously said:

"Never give in, never give in, never, never, never, never - in nothing, great or small, large or petty - never give in except to convictions of honor and good sense."

Epilogue:

"There Comes a Redeemer and He, Slowly Too, Fades Away"

Eyes of the World
Robert Hunter,
lyricist for the Grateful Dead

I HAVE PARKINSON'S. I was diagnosed at the ripe, old age of 48. I am finishing this at age 60. It's a progressive disease and its progress can't be stopped. The neurologist says that those of us who have "early onset" of the disease experience its march at a slower pace than those who get it at a more normal age (65+). I asked him what the chances were for a cure. His response: "Not in our lifetime."

Great. Here I am, fighting the battle God helped determine would be my lifetime pursuit and He's taking me out. I won't get into the theology of it all because little of it makes sense. But it's hard not to be pretty pissed off.

I could've been a damn good trial lawyer, one hell of an entrepreneur, maybe even a rock star (OK, that's a stretch).

But I sacrificed my family's financial well-being for years for the cause. I declined pay raises. We couldn't afford shit. We raised our kids in a modest twin home in a working class neighborhood, sent them to an urban school district where the kids look like the real world, not a suburban, La La Land cul-de-sac-loaded school district where the kids all look alike.

I'm figuring the disease will take me out before my normal retirement age. Maybe I'll make it to 65, maybe 63. But I'm not going to hang in there after my value to the agency has plummeted. I won't be the Brooks Robinson of Community Action Agencies (Brooks batted .200 in his last three seasons with the O's).

Some things are just more important than a cushy lifestyle.

If I could rewind to 1980 I'd do it all again.

Appendices

BB&T Acquisition of Susquehanna Bank and National Penn Bank

WELCOME TO THE LEHIGH VALLEY MARKET

The housing, community and economic development organizations of the Lehigh Valley welcome BB&T into the Lehigh Valley market. We are pleased that the bank has chosen the Lehigh Valley as its entry point into Pennsylvania.

We see the Community Reinvestment Act as a powerful tool to build a better community with more economic opportunity, better neighborhoods, a greater ability to accumulate assets and to ensure that all residents of the region prosper. But the effective use of that tool requires the housing, community and economic development organizations not to be observers, leaving the burden to the bank, but to be partners, sharing the responsibility with the financial services sector. We are anxious to work with BB&T as it joins us here in the Lehigh Valley market.

The groups listed at the bottom of this document propose a series of commitments that the bank might make in order to demonstrate the bank's intention to be an outstanding partner here, consistent with its outstanding community reinvestment performance in its Carolina home.

A GOOD START
We applaud the bank's establishment of a charitable foundation out of the proceeds of the transaction.

ECONOMIC AND SMALL BUSINESS DEVELOPMENT

Participate in the Lehigh Valley Economic Development Corporation's Lending Network, a regional network of economic development and commercial lenders designed to expedite access to credit in the promotion of business location and expansion in the region.

Use LVEDC as the "Certified Development Company" for any and all projects using the U.S. Small Business Administration's 504 loan program in Lehigh and Northampton counties.

Because financing urban and brownfield redevelopment is a special challenge and taking into account that there are numerous incentive financing programs available from the economic development community to assist in funding projects of this kind, the bank should make its best effort to utilize local incentive programs available through organizations like LVEDC, the Allentown Economic Development Corporation, Lehigh County Industrial Development Authority and Northampton County Industrial Development Authority (particularly their tax-exempt financing tools) where applicable, as they are designed to provide substantial incentives for the Bank's business clients to grow their business and expand their workforce in the region. Furthermore, these programs can enhance the bank's internal capacity, including its lenders' and underwriters' expertise, for financing such projects.

Invest at least $100,000 in The Rising Tide Community Loan Fund, the region's certified community development financial institution doing micro- and small business lending, at 1.5 percent.

Invest $25,000 in the Southside Bethlehem Keystone Innovation Zone, assisting start-up companies with technology-based grants and tax credit opportunities.

HOUSING

Develop underwriting policies that make it more difficult for owners of problem properties (properties that are tagged "unfit for human habitation") to buy more properties financed by the bank.

Commit to using federal Low-Income Housing Tax Credits to invest equity directly (rather than through a syndicator) in at least one new or preserved Lehigh Valley multi-family rental housing project.

Commit to using tax-free municipal financing tools as an additional mechanism for financing affordable rental housing.

Maintain Susquehanna Bank's part in the construction line of credit created by the Housing Association and Development Corporation of $500,000.

Hire in-house originators for the bank's mortgages rather than relying on brokers for that business.

Develop a competitive portfolio special mortgage product that includes financial counseling for low- to moderate-income homebuyers and buyers whose homes are located in LMI census tracts.

Maintain the commitment made by both National Penn and Susquehanna to a special mortgage product for LMI borrowers for low- to moderate-income buyers of Lehigh Valley Community Land Trust homes.

COMMUNITY DEVELOPMENT
Commit $300,000 per year for 10 years to one or more Neighborhood Partnership Programs in any of the three Lehigh Valley cities. (The tax credits from the Commonwealth of Pennsylvania, coupled with the federal deduction, will reduce the out-of-pocket expense to the bank to roughly $40,000.)

Prioritize urbanized communities for any new branches planned (Catasauqua, for example, should be a high priority).

Play a leadership role in the creation of a pool of "patient capital" of $1 million, committing at least $250,000 with a leadership investment.

Commit to keeping any branches in the cities or boroughs open for at least seven years (we understand that one of the two branches on Hamilton Street in Allentown's central business district is the exception); for any branches outside the cities and boroughs that the bank might close, give community and economic development groups and county and municipal officials at least four months' notice to enable them to explore alternatives.

CUSTOMER SERVICE AND INFRASTRUCTURE
Name a market leader in the Lehigh Valley.

Name a CRA/community development specialist whose geographic footprint is small enough to be effective (i.e., cutting the current staff complement would weaken the bank's ability to sustain at least the current effort).

Employ at least one Spanish-speaking mortgage originator.

Place bank decision-makers on the boards of directors of non-profits and quasi-public entities that can help the bank meet its CRA obligations.

Ensure that a fair proportion of the bank's charitable contributions support the community, economic and housing development infrastructure of the region. Also, maintain support for those organizations at the combined level of the two acquired banks.

Commit resources to provide special support to non-profits led by and serving primarily people of color, including mentoring, training and financial support designed to build those organizations' capacity to serve.

Commit the bank's wealth management division to participate as a pilot in the Water Fountain Project's "investment clubs," which will require financial planning advice for the club, administrative support and a match of participants' initial investment, up to a total of $5,000.

WILLING PARTNERS
The Lehigh Valley's community, economic and housing development organizations, listed below, are anxious to assist BB&T as it enters the Lehigh Valley marketplace.

- Allentown Economic Development Corporation
- Allentown Housing Authority
- Alliance for Building Communities
- Bethlehem Economic Development Corporation
- Community Action Committee of the Lehigh Valley
- Department of Community and Economic Development, City of Allentown
- Department of Community and Economic Development, City of Bethlehem
- Department of Community and Economic Development, City of Easton
- Department of Community and Economic Development, County of Lehigh
- Department of Community and Economic Development, County of Northampton
- Habitat for Humanity
- Housing Association and Development Corporation
- Lehigh Valley Economic Development Corporation
- Neighborhood Housing Service of the Lehigh Valley
- Northampton County Housing Authority
- Resurrected Life Community Development Corporation
- Valley Housing Development Corporation/Lehigh County Housing Authority

SAMPLE MEDIA ADVISORY

EVENT ADVISORY
31 January 2017

CONTACT: Alan L. Jennings
610-248-9900

DCED SECRETARY DAVIN TO JOIN SLATE BELT COMMUNITY LEADERS TO ANNOUNCE NEIGHBORHOOD PARTNERSHIP PROGRAM

Rural, Multi-Municipal Project is First of its Kind

The Community Action Committee of the Lehigh Valley (CACLV) will announce the approval of the first multi-municipal Neighborhood Partnership Program, "Slate Belt Rising," at a press conference on Thursday, February 2, at 1:30 PM. The briefing will take place at Bangor Trust Brewing, 11 Broadway, in Bangor.

The boroughs of Portland, Bangor, Pen Argyl, and Wind Gap will jointly plan and implement community revitalization initiatives through this six-year project. Corporate partners Merchants Bank of Bangor, Waste Management, ESSA Bank & Trust, and Lafayette Ambassador Bank have pledged a total of $775,000 to this project. In addition, the Northampton County Department of Community and Economic Development has committed $20,000 in federal Community Development Block Grant funding and $50,000 in Community Investment Partnership Program funding in the first year of the project.

The Neighborhood Partnership Program is a tax credit offered through the Pennsylvania Department of Community and Economic Development. Slate Belt Rising is CACLV's sixth Neighborhood Partnership Program following two in Allentown, two in Bethlehem, and one in Easton. It is also the first multi-municipal Neighborhood Partnership Program in the Commonwealth and the first to focus on the revitalization of boroughs. In part because of the groundbreaking nature of this project, Dennis Davin, Secretary of DCED, will be participating in the press conference.

Slate Belt Rising Steering Committee Chair Mike Ortoski will chair this event and will be joined by Pen Argyl Borough Manager Robin Zmoda, Secretary Davin, senior executives of the corporations investing in the project, Northampton County Executive John Brown and CACLV Executive Director Alan Jennings.

# # #

SAMPLE PRESS RELEASE

EVENT ADVISORY   CONTACT: Alan L. Jennings
31 January 2017   610-248-9900

FIRST MULTI-MUNICIPAL NEIGHBORHOOD PARTNERSHIP PROGRAM TO LAUNCH IN THE SLATE BELT

Community Action Committee of the Lehigh Valley (CACLV) announced the approval of the first multi-municipal Neighborhood Partnership Program in the Commonwealth of Pennsylvania, Slate Belt Rising, at a press conference held at the Bangor Bee Hive Community Center this afternoon.

The boroughs of Portland, Bangor, Pen Argyl, and Wind Gap will jointly plan and implement community revitalization initiatives through this six-year project. Slate Belt Rising will enhance inter-municipal cooperation to improve the appearance and utilization of commercial districts, upgrade the quality of the housing stock, increase homeownership, create opportunities for community engagement, and improve residential and commercial property values. The project's goals are to decrease the rates of crime, poverty, unemployment, and commercial and residential vacancies in the region.

During the first year, the program will focus its efforts in the Bangor business district. Specific projects will include two commercial façade improvements, four new business signs, and the installation of eight flower planters. The Portland business district will be improved during the project's second year. The program will also organize community building events, plant street trees, and fund youth development programs benefitting residents in all four boroughs. In addition, CACLV has committed to expanding its existing small business development and homeownership programs in the Slate Belt. A director will be hired in the next few weeks.

Two corporate sponsors, Waste Management and Merchants Bank of Bangor, have each committed $50,000 per year to Slate Belt Rising for a total of six years. In addition, ESSA Bank & Trust has committed $25,000 for the project's first year and Lafayette Ambassador Bank has committed a total of $25,000 over four years.

Speakers at the event included Slate Belt Rising Steering Committee Chair Mike Ortoski, CACLV Executive Director Alan L. Jennings, Northampton County Executive John Brown, State Senator Mario Scavello, Pen Argyl Borough Manager Robin Zmoda, Waste Management District Manager Scott Perin, and Merchants Bank of Bangor Senior Vice President and Chief Credit Officer Larry G. Rice, Jr.

The Neighborhood Partnership Program is a tax credit offered through the Pennsylvania Department of Community and Economic Development. In late December 2016, the commonwealth announced that $17.8 million in tax credits would be awarded to support 114 community investments through the umbrella Neighborhood Assistance Program. Slate Belt Rising is CACLV's sixth Neighborhood Partnership Program following two in Allentown, two in Bethlehem, and one in Easton. It is also the first multi-municipal Neighborhood Partnership Program in the Commonwealth and the first to focus on the revitalization of boroughs.

# # #

CACLV Values Statement

As an advocate, Community Action Committee of the Lehigh Valley (CACLV) is the economic and social justice conscience of the Lehigh Valley.

- We are partners, coalition-builders and team players.
- We are a think tank, conducting professional research on poverty and its causes, understanding issues as the first step in the problem-solving process.
- We define the cutting edge in the problem-solving process.
- We speak out, putting the truth above CACLV's institutional preservation.
- We believe charity is something a society must provide when there is no justice.
- We pursue justice.

As a community development organization, CACLV values neighborhoods that are economically self-sustainable.

- We want businesses to make a fair and honest profit in our neighborhoods.
- We want jobs to pay wages that enable households to be self-sufficient and are safe, enriching and in reasonable proximity to neighborhoods.
- We want institutions to be humane and responsive to human needs.
- We want neighborhoods to be culturally rich, fun and healthy.

- We want all people to participate in civic life and, indeed, we believe that citizenship is the highest form of self-sufficiency and that our society is far more threatened when poverty leads to apathy and dependence than when it leads to anger and activism.

As a human services agency, CACLV values people.

- We identify needs and push the community to respond rather than offer services based on available resources.
- We give people the tools to solve their own problems, rather than solve those problems for them.
- We treat people equally, with courtesy, compassion, respect, patience and dignity.
- We safeguard their confidentiality.
- We believe people deserve another chance but expect personal responsibility in taking advantage of that extra chance.

As a nonprofit corporation, CACLV values responsible stewardship of the funds entrusted to us and the resources available to us.

- We want our audits to be flawless.
- We want taxpayers and our donors to be certain that their funds are well-spent.
- We will not waste resources, including natural ones.
- We have a Board of Directors that has the highest standards for its fiduciary responsibility.

As an employer, CACLV values our employees.

- We respect the needs of our employees' families.
- We offer employment opportunities that are personally fulfilling.
- We try to pay fair wages and offer good benefits.
- We want the workplace to be safe.
- We value longevity, creativity, dedication, honesty and hard work.
- We are serious about equal opportunity and celebrate diversity.
- We have high standards of personal and professional conduct and ethics.
- We expect our employees to understand that they are role models.
- We respect our co-workers and treat them as we would want to be treated.
- We have fun.

A Manual on the Care and Feeding of CACLV's Volunteer Boards, Steering Committees, Advisory Boards and Task Forces

The mission of the Community Action Committee of the Lehigh Valley is to improve the quality of life in the Lehigh Valley by building a community in which all people have access to economic opportunities, the ability to pursue those opportunities, and a voice in the decisions that affect their lives.

Accomplishing this mission is made easier by the participation of scores of volunteers who perform a variety of tasks. There is no task more important than the work of this agency's volunteer boards, steering committees, advisory boards, and task forces.

GOVERNANCE AND COMPOSITION
The creation of a non-profit corporation requires the establishment of a board of directors charged with ultimate fiduciary and programmatic authority and responsibility. The Economic Opportunity Act of 1964 provided for the development of a new local agency, funded in part by the federal government, whose governing body, the board of directors, would provide for "maximum feasible participation" by public officials, private citizens, and members or representatives of the low-income community in which the agency does its work.

Maximum feasible participation, a voice in the decisions that affect all of us, is just one of the concepts that the Community Action Committee of the Lehigh Valley (CACLV) employs as it works with and for its board of directors, boards of subsidiary corporations, and a variety of steering committees, advisory boards, and, as needed, task forces. At CACLV, the board has both the ultimate authority and responsibility for the agency. Deference to the decisions and recommendations of the board and its members is a mandate for all staff members.

To enhance the work of the board and staff, CACLV's board of directors often defers some aspects of leadership to other entities. Most significantly, the boards of directors of CACLV's four subsidiary corporations enjoy nearly complete autonomy except for two or three important constraints. The bylaws of the subsidiaries, the Community Action Development Corporation of the Lehigh Valley d.b.a. the Community Action Development Corporation of Allentown, the Community Action Development Corporation of Bethlehem, the Rising Tide Community Loan Fund, and the Lehigh Valley Community Land Trust, stipulate that the CACLV board appoints members to these corporate boards. By inference, then, CACLV's board may also dismiss the boards or members of the boards. In addition, the subsidiary organizations must submit any bylaws changes to the board of CACLV for approval. Finally, each individual subsidiary may have additional constraints with respect to CACLV's board; staff and board members need to be familiar with the bylaws of each corporation.

In somewhat similar fashion, CACLV has also deferred a measure of responsibility and authority to steering committees, advisory boards, and task forces. However, the decisions of these entities are subject to review and eventual approval, or disapproval, by the CACLV board. Ultimate fiduciary and programmatic authority rests with the CACLV board of directors in all matters.

The composition of the board is also critical to the fulfillment of CACLV's mission. The CACLV board is "tri-partite" by federal law. One-third of the board represents low-income people; low-income people are encouraged to become members of the board. One-third of the board comes from the public at large and one-third of the board consists of elected public officials currently in office or their designees.

Subsidiary corporations have their own stipulations about the composition of their boards. At least half of the members of the boards of the Community Action Development Corporation of the Lehigh Valley and the Community Action Development Corporation of Bethlehem must be residents of the targeted neighborhoods; the Lehigh Valley Community Land Trust has a tri-partite board with one sector made up of people who own land trust homes.

Most boards have their own constituencies who should be represented but the need for diversity that draws members from a broad cross section of the community is a feature of every board associated with CACLV. Boards should develop a description of optimal board composition, making certain that the membership reflects racial, ethnic, and gender diversity. This description will guide the recruitment of new members.

CACLV DEFINITIONS
Board of directors: a governing body that has fiduciary authority and responsibility for a corporation. The board authorizes the creation of other steering committees and advisory boards.

Steering committee: an oversight committee that provides assistance with program development, guidance for decision-making, and help with fundraising and budget development. Steering committees are usually made up of high level stakeholders such as government or private funders and provide connections among stakeholders for collaborative relationships. A steering committee makes recommendations to the board that created it.

Advisory board: a committee of volunteers who have an interest in the cause or expertise or other resources that they bring with them. An advisory board typically focuses on one program in the agency and makes recommendations to the board that created it.

Task force: a group of individuals who are appointed to work on a single defined task or activity; the group disbands when the task has been completed. A task force makes recommendations to the board that created it.

Note: for purposes of this document, boards, steering committees, advisory boards, task forces, and other advisory groups will be called "boards."

Subsidiary corporation: at CACLV, a corporation formed by CACLV to achieve a purpose of CACLV; this corporation is autonomous except as specified in its corporate bylaws.

Committee: a group of volunteers that is appointed by a board, steering committee, or advisory board, to provide guidance on a particular aspect of a program. Committees may be "standing" or "ad hoc." Ad hoc is a Latin term meaning "for this." At CACLV, committees, even those that function regularly over a long period of time, are more likely to be ad hoc; if there are standing committees, their functions are noted in the bylaws or other written policies. CACLV typically limits standing committees to avoid changing bylaws when committees are changed or new committees are created.

A board meets regularly according to a predetermined schedule approved by its members. Boards set a pattern for date and time of their meetings, e.g., at 3:30 p.m., on the third Wednesday of every month. Task forces and committees meet as needed although some task forces and committees may designate a regularly-scheduled date and time.

BYLAWS AND OTHER GUIDING DOCUMENTS

Every board of directors has bylaws; these are the rules of the organization that must be written prior to incorporation and filed with the Pennsylvania Department of State along with the request for incorporation. Bylaws may differ in content but, at a minimum, they should include:
- the name of the corporation (even if the organization does not commonly use that name);
- a mission statement or statement of purpose;
- a non-discrimination statement;
- the time frame for the annual meeting;
- specifics about the governing body;
- a policy regarding conflict of interest;
- a statement regarding indemnification;

- a process for amending the bylaws; and
- a process for dissolution of the corporation.

An annual meeting is a mandate for all boards of directors incorporated in the Commonwealth of Pennsylvania; the time frame for scheduling the meeting is stated in the bylaws, e.g., during a particular quarter of the fiscal year or in a particular month.

Within the bylaws' description of the board of directors, specifics will include:
- a description of those who are eligible or mandated to sit on the board;
- the term of office of each member;
- the number of terms that may be served consecutively;
- the procedure for electing, appointing or removing board members;
- a list of the board officers with their terms of office
- a description of the duties of each officer.

Governing boards that are not boards of directors, such as steering committees and advisory boards may have rules that are similar to bylaws and should contain information similar to the content of bylaws. Statements about indemnification and dissolution may not be necessary.

STAFF RESPONSIBILITIES

Staff members serve as resources for the volunteer boards and committees; they are not members of the boards and they do not have a vote in decision-making. Staff will offer assistance as needed or requested. Usually, staff will record minutes or notes of a meeting. Room reservations, refreshments, and any other considerations for the meeting space are staff responsibilities. Staff is also charged with developing agendas, raising issues, and providing background for deliberations. At all times, staff will defer to the members and implement the decisions of the governing entity.

Staff members are responsible for the records of board membership. In addition to the usual basic information such as addresses and phone numbers, staff should record the date that the board member was seated and the end date for that person's term. If a new board member replaces a board member who has not completed his/her term, staff should note who was replaced and assign that person's term end to the newly-appointed board member. Upon completion of the partial term, the board member is entitled to as many full terms as the bylaws allow.

Prior to every meeting of a board, steering committee, advisory board, or committee, staff will consult with the presiding officer regarding the agenda, information needed for decision-making, and the expectations of the meeting. At CACLV, staff should provide copies of any and all public notices and press clippings regarding the corporation, the board, or staff at the meeting. Staff members, in consultation with the presiding officer, will compose motions for the board's actions. If a committee has not met prior to the distribution of the board packet, staff may compose draft motions that the committee may decide to recommend. A disclaimer should be included with the motions as follows: (The [name of the] committee motions were developed prior to the committee's meeting. Final language and documents will be provided at the Board meeting.)

Resource persons and directors of programs are encouraged to be in touch with board members as issues arise. Because decision-making is dependent on having complete factual information, staff members can assist board members by discussing all aspects of the issues with the presiding officer and/or other board members. At the same time, staff members will find it helpful to identify and work with board members who will support staff recommendations and are willing to "go out on a limb" with staff. Staff members are seen by board members as the people who are closest to the program and the issues that arise; staff members, especially directors of programs or functions, need to learn the "politics" of boards and how to make those politics work for the good of the program.

Staff do not chair meetings nor do they dominate discussion; the board meeting is a meeting of the volunteers, not the staff. Ideally, staff "speak when spoken to" or report as requested by the Board except for the top staff person attending the meeting. Staff do not sit at the Board table unless invited to do so. Staff members need to remember that boards can make decisions about budgets, programs, and personnel matters. Staff need to respect the board's role and to be extremely cautious in their interactions with board members. Open defiance is never acceptable.

At the same time, staff need to be alert to concerns that may arise. A board member has a duty of trust and loyalty. He/she is expected to leave the board meeting and support the actions that have been determined in a democratic process. In addition, board members are to avoid conflicts of interest; they are expected to disclose any conflicts, or potential conflicts, to their fellow board members. If a staff person is concerned that there are issues arising, either of trust and loyalty or conflicts of interest, the staff person has an obligation to report that concern to CACLV's Executive Director.

MEETINGS
To prepare for a meeting of any board, staff will prepare an agenda and any other supporting materials to be distributed to the members of that group; it is important for the smooth functioning of each board that these documents be circulated, by email or postal mail, with sufficient lead time, usually a week, for members to prepare themselves for the meeting. A few copies of the board packet should be available at the meeting. Each month, one full board packet should be kept on file in the corporate office of CACLV or in the subsidiary corporation's files. Advisory boards and steering committees will have board packets that are similar to corporate board packets; full packets should be on file in the CACLV office and in the program's files.

Included in board packets will be 1) a meeting notice and agenda for the upcoming meeting; 2) minutes or notes of the board's most recent previous meeting; 3) anticipated or proposed action items (motions); 4) fiscal reports; 5) background information for any discussion or action item; and 6) program reports. From month to month, these documents should have a consistent "look" that includes keeping the documents in the same order, printing them in the same font, and formatting them in the same way.

When preparing a board agenda, staff members should remember to include the following items:
- Call to Order
- Approval of Minutes
- Review of Financials
- President's Report

- Executive Director's Report and/or Director's Report or Staff Report
- Committee Reports
- Privilege of the Floor
- Adjournment

Committees should be listed on the agenda only if they have a report or motions that will be presented at the meeting. It is not necessary to call for Old Business or New Business on agendas; all business should arise from the documents presented and/or the staff and committee reports.

Prior to the distribution of the board packet, staff will call, email, or meet with the presiding officer and any other volunteers critical to the conduct of the meeting. Agendas must be approved by the presiding officer who will run the meeting. Issues that will be raised at the meeting should be part of this preparatory discussion. It is essential that the volunteers are fully briefed and fully engaged in the work of the board.

Minutes are the record of the proceedings of the board; every corporate board is required to keep minutes. Although staff may prepare the minutes, the secretary of the board is responsible for the minutes and indicates that responsibility by signing an "official" document. Minutes are a corporate record of decisions made; there is no need for minutes to record everything that is said.

Minutes need to include:
- the name of the organization and the date and time the board met (and adjourned);
- attendance of board members, staff, and guests and a list of the board members who were excused or absent;
- the kind of meeting, e.g., regular or special, or annual;
- the name of the person who presided;
- the approval of the previous meeting's minutes (by board vote);
- a brief description of board, staff, or committee reports that were presented;
- all motions, formatted for easy reference, and the outcome of the vote.

The minutes should indicate that a motion was made and seconded and the fact that the motion was approved or disapproved. Although it is not required that the names of the person who made the motion and the person who seconded the motion be recorded, it is a courtesy to note their involvement in the action. It is not necessary to record motions that were withdrawn or otherwise disregarded. The inclusion of a brief background on a motion is helpful so that, in the future, it will be clear why the board took this action.

A complete file of signed minutes must be kept by each corporation. Each year, CACLV and its subsidiaries are audited by an outside fiscal auditing firm; the auditors will review the corporate minutes. In addition, the annual monitoring of some contracts, such as the Community Services Block Grant contract, includes a review of the corporate minutes.

Many committees appreciate having a record of their discussions. These notes, prepared by staff, are not required except as the board members request them. For instance, there are no notes prepared after the meetings of the CACLV Board's committees.

In most cases, meetings are conducted according to Robert's Rules of Order (See Appendix A). Committees and task forces may choose to conduct meetings less formally and will usually reach decisions by consensus rather than formal voting. For the more formal meetings, presiding chairs should be familiar with the basics of parliamentary procedure but, if they are not, staff will need to provide assistance to guarantee the smooth disposition of business. Written guidance is available.

COMMITTEES

Most boards create committees in order to thoroughly vet issues and accomplish tasks on behalf of the corporation and/or the board. These committees can be created in the bylaws or guidelines or by Board fiat. Bylaws name the "standing" committees, those committees that are necessary and cannot be discontinued without an amendment of the bylaws. All Board members are expected to serve on at least one committee. When other committees are created by the board, the motion creating these committees should note if there is an intended end date for the life of the committee.

At CACLV, standing committees are rare. Typically, there is an Executive Committee consisting, minimally, of the officers of the corporation and a Nominating or Board Development Committee that is charged with developing a slate of officers for the board. Because the functions of these committees are specified in the bylaws, the committees themselves must be named as standing committees.

Executive committees at CACLV meet infrequently. The democratic process that governs all boards can be threatened if a small group of board members meets frequently and begins to make decisions without consultation with other members of the board. Even if others are consulted, what Alan Jennings calls "a ruling junta" can be created and other board members can become a "rubber stamp" body. Of course, there are times when timely action is required and the Executive Committee may be convened for that purpose. All of the bylaws of CACLV and its subsidiaries stipulate that any action taken by the Executive Committee must be ratified by the full membership at the next meeting of the board. Although there has never been an instance of a board's failing to ratify an Executive Committee's decision, the potential exists. Each board will have to determine what it should do in that event. An Executive Committee should be in tune with the wishes of the board and be able to take an action that is likely to be approved by the board. Failure to approve an action could be seen as a sign of other problems within the board. It is acceptable to amend the bylaws so that the board is to be informed of the Executive Committee's decision but does not need to ratify it.

With the acceptance of electronic voting by email, the need for Executive Committee decision-making has diminished. Permission to conduct voting electronically must be noted in the bylaws. When board members receive motions by email, those voting should be encouraged to "reply to all" to ensure that all directors are seeing the exchange, including questions asked, concerns raised and objections voiced so that directors are not voting in a vacuum.

A Board Development or Nominating Committee is charged with assuring that all allocated slots on the board are filled. To accomplish this task, the Committee recruits new board members to be elected at the corporation's annual meeting.

This Committee has primary responsibility for maintaining the racial, ethnic, and gender diversity of the board. Throughout the year, it may be necessary to replace board members who resign or are removed from the board.

The Board Development or Nominating Committee develops a slate of officers for election at the annual meeting.

Board recruitment by committee or staff member should include an honest assessment of the responsibilities to be undertaken by the new board member or officer. It is not helpful to minimize the amount of work involved. Worthy candidates do not want to join boards that have little activity or little opportunity to make a difference. Board members who are told that there is little to do are likely to do little. Rather, board members should be challenged, engaged and actively involved in the work of the agency.

Newly appointed board members should be invited to an orientation session that is usually conducted by staff. Other board members may wish to participate. The Board Development or Nominating Committee should assure that orientation of new members occurs.

Other committees are appointed by the presiding officer who will ascertain the preferences for service of the members. A chair or two co-chairs will be appointed by the presiding officer and the members of the committee will set meeting dates and times. Setting a regular time, date, and meeting place for committees makes it easier for both board and staff to fulfill committee obligations. Efforts should be made to encourage the participation of low-income members and community representatives by reasonable accommodations to their work schedules and other availability. It is an appropriate use of agency resources to pay certain expenses for low-income Board members in order to ensure their participation, including transportation and child care costs.

At least one staff person serves as a resource to each board and committee. That person provides minutes, notes, and other documentation as requested and consults with the committee leadership in advance of each meeting. At least a week prior to the meeting, staff members will review the business of the committee with the chair of the meeting. A printed agenda will be developed and distributed to the members of the committee and the president of the board.

Committees do not vote nor are their decisions binding unless the board has given authority for that decision-making. Quorum for a committee is two members. Committees make recommendations to the full board; those recommendations are included as action items noted, by committee, in the board packet for the full board meeting.

Community volunteers are generally welcome on Board committees. However, they should not serve as chair.

APPENDIX A

ROBERT'S RULES
Here are some basics from Robert's Rules, a traditional and highly-regarded system for conducting business. The purpose of these codified procedures is twofold: 1) to enable a democratic process that ensures the participation of everyone who wants to participate (and the exclusion of those who are not eligible to participate) and 2) to move the meeting along in an efficient, orderly fashion. Parliamentary procedure should not be seen as a rigid system that is daunting to the presiding officer or detrimental to the flow of the meeting. Rather, it is meant to provide consistently-run meetings in which all have an opportunity to be heard and to have a role in the decisions that are made.

The chair, or presiding officer, is expected to maintain order, calling on individuals who want to speak and making sure that all who want to speak have an opportunity. Presiding officers may decide against calling on a person who has already spoken twice on a motion or who appears to be attempting to dominate the conversation.

In order to conduct business, the board designates the number of people who must be present for a vote to take place; this is a quorum. The board's bylaws define the quorum of the deliberative body. At CACLV, a board quorum is usually at least fifty (50) percent of the non-vacant seats on the board; for committees, the quorum is two (2) committee members. Any other definition of quorum should take into consideration the need to ensure the participation of the greatest number of board members.

The chair is responsible to determine if a quorum is present. If a quorum does not exist, the chair should recognize a motion to adjourn and, if necessary, to set a date for a subsequent meeting to conduct urgent business; the motion requires a second and a vote by the body. Following adjournment, the board can choose to hear reports and engage in informal discussion but no votes may be taken. If a quorum of the Executive Committee is present, the Committee can be convened to deal with urgent business items.

The decisions of the board are made through motions presented to the body by its members. An individual or a committee may bring a motion to the floor. If the motion has been made by an individual, another board member must "second" the motion. Seconding the motion is an indication that the person seconding thinks a motion should be discussed; it does not imply assent to the motion. If the motion is coming from a committee that held an official meeting at which there was a quorum, the motion is considered to be seconded at the time that it is presented to the board; therefore, it is not necessary to obtain a second to a committee motion.

Motions should be presented prior to any discussion of the matter at hand. The chair will say something like, "a motion has been made and seconded to …. Is there any discussion? When discussion seems to be ending, the chair will ask if the board is ready to vote. The chair will ask that all those in favor indicate by saying "aye" or "yes", by standing, by raising a hand or, rarely, by written ballot. In similar fashion, the chair will ask for those voting against the motion and those abstaining from the motion. At CACLV, a majority of those present and voting are needed to pass or defeat a motion; an abstention is a zero vote. The vote is recorded in the minutes; however, it is not necessary to record the count. Anyone abstaining may request that his/her abstention be recorded in the minutes but it is not necessary. Frequently, a board member will abstain because of a conflict of interest; he or she may wish to avoid any perception of inappropriate participation in a decision of the board.

When a discussion is protracted, a member of the board may "call the question" (or "call the previous question"). The chair is required to halt discussion and take a vote to determine if board members are ready to vote or want to continue discussion. There can be no discussion of this motion. The motion to call the question must receive a 2/3 majority of the members present and voting. If the vote is in the affirmative, the chair calls for the vote on the original motion immediately; if the vote is negative, discussion continues.

Meetings of CACLV boards are open to the public and media; therefore, deliberations should be open and transparent. Nevertheless, there are items of business, such as real estate transactions and personnel actions, that should be conducted outside the public eye. When the business of the matter is sensitive or confidential, a member of the board may move that the board go into executive session. The motion must be seconded. The motion is adopted by majority vote. Anyone who is not a board member should be asked to leave the meeting unless they are needed for the board's deliberations. Executive session discussions are not recorded in the minutes of the meeting; if they are to be recorded, the minutes are separate and can be approved only in executive session. Members and anyone else present are bound to maintain confidentiality regarding executive session discussions. The minutes of the regular meeting will record the motion to go into executive session and the motion to end the executive session. With direction from the board, decisions approved in executive session may be recorded in the minutes of the regular meeting. Disciplinary action that affects a member of the board is always discussed in executive session.

A motion to adjourn must be made and seconded; the motion is not debatable. A vote is taken and the meeting either continues or is adjourned.

A meeting can be adjourned without a motion in a body that normally completes its business at each meeting (as CACLV's boards do). The presiding officer asks if there is any additional business. If there is none, the chair can declare the adjournment.